D1611933

THE FATHERS OF THE CHURCH

A NEW TRANSLATION

VOLUME 67

THE FATHERS OF THE CHURCH

A NEW TRANSLATION

NOVATIAN

THE TRINITY
THE SPECTACLES · JEWISH FOODS
IN PRAISE OF PURITY
LETTERS

Translated by

RUSSELL J. DE SIMONE, O.S. A

Villanova University
Augustinian Institute, Villanova University
Patristic Institute "Augustinianum"
of the Lateran Pontifical University, Rome

THE CATHOLIC UNIVERSITY OF AMERICA PRESS
Washington, D.C.

Nihil Obstat:

JOSEPH B. COLLINS, S.S., S.T.D.
Censor Librorum

Imprimatur:

PATRICK CARDINAL A. O'BOYLE, D.D.
Archbishop of Washington

June 12, 1972

The *nihil obstat* and *imprimatur* are official declarations that a book or pamphlet is free of doctrinal or moral error. No implication is contained therein that those who have granted the *nihil obstat* and the *imprimatur* agree with content, opinions, or statements expressed.

Library of Congress Cataloging in Publication Data

Novatianus.
  The Trinity, The spectacles, Jewish foods, In praise of purity, Letters.

  (The Fathers of the church, a new translation, v. 67)
  1. Trinity—Early works to 1800. 2. Christian ethics—Early church. I. DeSimone, Russell J., tr. II. Title. III. Series.
  BR65.N62E5 1973   230'.1'3   73-9872
  ISBN 0-8132-0067-9

TO THE MEMORY OF MY FATHER
AND TO MY MOTHER

CONTENTS

SELECT GENERAL BIBLIOGRAPHY*

Amann, E. "Novatien et novatianisma," DTC 11 (1931) 816-49.
Ayerst, D., and Fisher, A.S.T. *Records of Christianity* 1 (New York 1971).
Casamassa, A. *Noviziano* (Dispense universitarie; Rome 1949).
Cathélinaud, N. *L'église Novatienne de Rome. Etude topographique, archéologique et prosopographique.* Paris: Diplôme d'études supé-rieures de Lettres (1960/61).
Daniélou, J., and Marrou, H.-I. *The Christian Centuries: The First Six Hundred Years* I (New York 1964).
DeSimone, R. *The Treatise of Novatian the Roman Presbyter on the Trinity: A Study of the Text and the Doctrine* (Studia Ephemeridis "Augustinianum" 4, Rome 1970).
Diercks, G. F. "Novatien et son temps," in his *Novatiani opera . . .* (CCL 4; Turnhout 1972) viii-xiii.
Frutaz, A. P. "Novaziano, Cimitero detto di," EC 8 (1952) 1974-76.
Harnack, A. "Novatian, Novatianism," *New Schaff-Herzog Encyclopedia* 8 (1953) 197-202.
Mohrmann, C. "Les origines de la latinité chrétienne à Rome," *Vigiliae Christianae* 3 (1949) 67-106, 163-83; repr. in her *Études sur le latin des chrétiens* 3 (Storia e letteratura 103; Rome 1965) 67-126.
Peterson, E. "Novaziano e Novazianismo," EC 8 (1952) 1976-80.
Quasten, J. *Patrology* 2 (Westminster, Md., 1953) 212-15.
Vogt, H. J. *Coetus Sanctorum: Der Kirchenbegriff des Novatian und die Geschichte seiner Sonderkirche* (Bonn 1968).
Walker, G. S. M. *The Churchmanship of St. Cyprian* (Richmond, Va., 1969).

*Texts and translations are listed in the separate bibliographies for the several works of Novatian.

ABBREVIATIONS

ACW   *Ancient Christian Writers* (Westminister, Md.-London 1946-).

CCL   *Corpus christianorum.* Series latina (Turnhout 1953-).

CSEL   *Corpus scriptorum ecclesiasticorum latinorum* (Vienna 1866-).

DTC   *Dictionnaire de théologie catholique,* ed. A. Vacant *et al.* (Paris 1903-50).

EC   *Enciclopedia cattolica* (Vatican City 1946-57).

FC   *The Fathers of the Church: A New Translation* (New York [afterwards Washington, D.C.] 1947-).

GCS   *Die griechischen christlichen Schriftsteller der ersten drei Jahrhunderte* (Leipzig 1897-).

NCE   *New Catholic Encyclopedia* (New York 1967).

PG   J.-P. Migne, *Patrologia graeca.*

PL   J.-P. Migne, *Patrologia latina.*

GENERAL INTRODUCTION

HROUGH HIS COMPOSITION of *The Trinity* in the middle of the third century, Novatian has the distinction of being the first Roman theologian to write a theological treatise in Latin and so becomes a pioneer and founder of Roman Latin theology. This is an eminence that to some extent stands apart from the administrative importance his ability won him in the Roman church of that time. His outstanding position there may by judged from his standing at Rome after Pope Fabian's martyrdom in A. D. 250. As presbyter Novatian had charge during the vacancy of the see and wrote in the name of the church at Rome to churches throughout the world. Of such letters, however, only three—albeit important ones—survive.[1] Thus we do not have an adequate body of primary documents from which to illustrate fully Novatian's central importance for the Church at a brief crisis in her history and his valuable contribution to it. History tends to emphasize rather the immediately succeeding years, which brought Novatian, as antipope, into contumacious opposition to the duly elected bishop of Rome.

The greatest of the historians of the early Church, Eusebius of Caesarea, calls Novatian *Novatus,* and later Greek writers have the forms *Navatus* and *Novatus;*[2] his real name, however, was *Novatianus.* This is quite evident, not only from the works of Cyprian and Dionysius of Alexandria (contemporaries of Novatian), but also on

---

1 The three letters survived among the correspondence of Cyprian (*Epp.* 30, 31, 36 [CSEL 3.2.549-64, 572-75]); henceforth, we shall refer to them as Novatian, *Ep.* 1, 2, 3 respectively.

2 Eusebius, *Historia ecclesiastica* 6.43(GCS 9².612; tr. by R.J. Deferrari, FC 29.78 and n. 1); Photius, *Bibliotheca* Cod. 182 (PG 103.531D; ed. R. Henry, *Photius: Bibliothèque* [Paris 1960] 2.192; henceforth, Henry); Epiphanius, *Panarion* 59 (GCS 31.363); Theodoret of Cyr(rh)us, *Haereticarum fabularum compendium* 3.5 (PG 83.406C).

1

the testimony of Ambrose, Jerome, and other later sources.[3] The
two names were confused because a Novatus who was a priest of
Carthage and an adversary of Cyprian was involved with Novatian in
the schism against Pope Cornelius.

We do not know the exact date of his birth. He must have been
born either at the end of the second century or at the beginning of
the third century, that is, about 190-210, since at the middle of the
third century he was already an outstanding priest of the Roman
Church and very active.

Plotius, in his extracts of now lost works of Philostorgius, reports
the latter's claim that Novatian was born in Phrygia. Photius himself,
however, does not know where Philostorgius received his informa-
tion.[4] Such a statement was probably due to a certain tendency to
link Novatian's doctrine with Montanist rigorism. Authors give
Rome, or at least Italy, as the place of his birth.[5]

We know practically nothing of Novatian's early years. Before his
conversion, which took place at a mature age, he was a Stoic philo-
sopher.[6] A circumstantial account of how Novatian came into the
Church is given by Pope Cornelius in writing to Fabius bishop of
Antioch.[7]

> The occasion of his having accepted the faith was Satan, who
> entered him and dwelt in him for a long time; when he was being
> healed by the exorcists he fell into a severe illness and, being

---

3 Cyprian, *Epp.* 44.1; 47.1; 52.1; 55.1, 2, 3, 5, 24; 59.9; 60.3; 68.1 (CSEL
  3.2.597 etc.; FC 51.112 etc.); Dionysius of Alexandria, Letter to Novatian
  (Eusebius, *Hist. eccl.* 6.45 [GCS 9².626; FC 29.87]); *id.*, Letter to Dionysius of Rome (Eusebius, *op. cit.* 7.8 [GCS 9². 646; FC 29.99]; (Ambrose,
  De paenitentia 1.3.10 (*bis*), 3.14 (*bis*) (CSEL 83.123, 124, 126) etc.; Jerome,
  De viris ill. 70 (PL 23.681; ed. E. Richardson, *Texte und Untersuchungen*
  14.1 [Leipzig 1896] 39).
4 Philostorgius, *Hist. eccl.* 8.15 (GCS 21.115).
5 E. Peterson, "Novaziano e Novazianismo," EC 8 (1952) 1976; C.
  Mohrmann, "Les origines de la latinité chrétienne à Rome," *Vigiliae Christianae* 3 (1949) 163 (*Etudes* . . . 3.106).
6 Cyprian, *Ep.* 55.16 (FC 51.143), 60.3 (FC 51.195). Cf. Casamassa,
  Novaziano 233, 252-54.
7 Eusebius, *Hist. eccl.* 6.43 (FC 29.78-86, esp. 79). Eusebius knew (*locc.
  citt.*) two other letters of Cornelius to Fabius concerning Novatian but
  does not quote from them.

considered as all but dead, received baptism by affusion on the
very bed where he lay, if, indeed, one should say that such a man
received it. However, he did not receive the other things, after he
had escaped his illness, which one must share according to the
canon of the Church, including the being sealed by the bishop.[8]
Subsequently Novatian was ordained a priest, despite the opposition
of "all the clergy and many of the laity, on the ground that it was
not possible for one who had been baptized by affusion in bed
because of sickness as this fellow to be ordained to an order. . . ."[9]
Although baptism on a sickbed, so-called clinical baptism, was valid
in the eyes of the Church,[10] it rendered Novatian irregular for
ordination. An exception was made in Novatian's case by Pope Cornelius' predecessor, probably Pope Fabian. "But it is hardly cred-
ible," observes H. Weyer, that Novatian's "ordination was performed
despite the opposition of the clergy and many of the laity."[11] It is
true that Cornelius speaks of Novatian's craftiness and duplicity, his
perjuries, falsehoods, and unsociability; nevertheless, the same
Cornelius—sarcastically, of course, but not without reason—calls him
a "marvelous fellow" and "this dogmatist, champion of the Church's
doctrine."[12] We must bear in mind that Cornelius paints a rather
repulsive picture of Novatian in his letter to Fabius, bishop of Antioch, to discourage the latter from siding with Novatian. Upon
critical examination, we find that many of the charges were seemingly based on malicious gossip.[13] Practically everything we know about
Novatian was written by his adversaries, whose statements about him
are bound to be tinged with passion and prejudice. Harnack justly
observes, "the fact of his ordination, as well as the evidence of his
enemies, goes to show that he enjoyed a great reputation not only
for learning and eloquence but also for virtue."[14] In fact, the *Ad*

8 Eusebius, *Hist. eccl.* 6.43 (FC 29.83-84).
9 Eusebius, *Hist. eccl.* 6.43 (FC 29. 84-85).
10 Cf. Cyprian, *Ep.* 69.12-17 (CSEL 3.2.760-65; FC 51.252-57).
11 H. Weyer, "Novatian and Novatianism," NCE 10.534.
12 Eusebius, *Hist. eccl.* 6.43 *passim* (FC 29.79-81).
13 J. Quasten, *Patrology* 2.237; É. Amann, "Novatien et Novatianisme," DTC
   11 (1931) 892.
14 A Harnack, "Novatian, Novatianism," *New Schaff-Herzog Encyclopedia* 8
   (1953) 199.

Novatianum (253-57 A. D.), a polemic against Novatian, states:

> that as long as Novatian was is the Church of Christ, he wept over the sins of his neighbors as if they were his own, bore the burdens of his brethren, as the Apostle exhorts, and strengthened with his exhortations those who were weak in divine faith.[15]

It is also interesting to note that about a century later, Canon XII of the NeoCaesarean Council (314-25) states:

> If anyone was baptized while he was gravely ill, he cannot be promoted to the dignity of the priesthood, since such faith is not due to personal conviction but springs from necessity. However, such a person may be admitted to orders later, if he shows signs of personal conviction and faith and if there be a dearth of men.[16]

During March of 251, the persecution of Decius slackened when the emperor was obliged to leave Rome to face two rivals. Since the see of Rome had been vacant for one year, sixteen bishops assembled there and elected Cornelius bishop of Rome in preference to Novatian. Novatian refused to acknowledge Cornelius as bishop and had himself consecrated a bishop by three South Italian bishops whom Novatian had put into confinement, "and at the tenth hour, when they were drunk and sick therefrom, he compelled them by force by a counterfeit and vain imposition of the hands to confer the episcopate upon him. . . ."[17]

Disappointed in his ambition to become bishop of Rome, Novatian set himself up as antipope and champion of the rigoristic party which would deny reconciliation to the lapsed and consecrate him bishop of Rome. He accused Cornelius of being a *libellaticus* (one who had not actually sacrificed to the gods but had secured a written statement [*libellus*] that he had done so) and of having been in communion with bishops who had offered such sacrifice.[18] Among

15 Anonymous, *Ad Novatianum* 13.8 (CSEL 3.3.63.9; CCL 4.147).
16 C. Kirch, *Enchiridion fontium historiae ecclesiasticae antiquae* (Barcelona 1960) 388; J. Mansi, *Sacrorum conciliorum nova et amplissima collectio* (repr. 1960 Graz) 2.541.
17 Eusebius, *Hist. eccl.* 6.43 (FC 29.81).
18 Cf. Cyprian, *Ep.* 55.10 (CSEL 3.2.631; FC 51.140).

Novatian's adherents were clerics and Roman confessors, who later, however, returned to the bosom of the true Church.[19] In order to prevent his followers from deserting him, Cornelius says that when Novatian had made the offerings and was giving out Holy Communion he forced his followers to swear: "I will not return to Cornelius."[20]

Novatian accused Cornelius of laxity through favoring the readmission to the Church of those who had apostatized during the Decian persecution. According to H.J. Vogt, "for Novatian the Church is, above all, the grand common 'We' of all the faithful..."[21] J. Daniélou however, maintains that the Church was for Novatian a select group of spiritually minded people, a Church of prophets and martyrs.[22] So as not contaminate his Church, he denied reconciliation to the lapsed and would not readmit them to the Church under any condition, since he claimed that no one but God had the power to forgive them their sins. Sinners were to be exhorted to repent and to do penance, but their pardon was to be left to God, who alone had the right to grant it.[23] Novatian had clearly contradicted himself. He admitted, right from the beginning of the controversy, the possibility of reconciliation for the lapsed. In his Letter 1, Novatian did not oppose the reconciliation of the lapsed, but only their premature reconciliation. He considered their desire for reconciliation as lawful.[24] He agreed to the reconciliation of those in danger of death who had not yet done full penance. He reversed his initial position and denied that the Church had the right to condone apostasy even at the moment of death. Cyprian did not

19 Cyprian, *Ep.* 51.1 (CSEL 3.2.614; FC 51.126).

20 Eusebius, *Hist. eccl.* 6.43 (FC 29.85).

21 Cf. H. J. Vogt, *Coetus Sanctorum: Der Kirchenbegriff des Novatian und die Geschichte seiner Sonderkirche* (Bonn 1968) 83-86, esp. his words, "Für Novatian ist die Kirche zunächst das grosse gemeinsame 'Wir' aller Gläubigen, der Rahmen ihres Lebens, Denkens und Handelns" (p.83).

22 J. Daniélou and Henri Marrou, *The Christian Centuries: The First Six Hundred Years* 1 (New York 1964) 199; henceforth, *The Christian Centuries*.

23 Cf. Socrates, *Hist. eccl.* 4.28 (PG 67.538B); Cyprian, *Ep.* 55.26-27 (CSEL 3.2.644-46; FC 51.150-52).

24 Novatian, *Ep.* 1.7 (ed. Diercks, CCL 4.205); commonly cited as [Cyprian,] *Ep.* 30.

fail to indicate Novatian's inconsistency; he tolerated defrauders and adulterers in his Church but at the same time unmercifully rejected the lapsed.[25] Novatian and his party were excommunicated by a Roman synod in 251, which settled the question of the lapsed.[26]

Novatian's later years are lost in obscurity. G. F. Diercks appears to distrust the indications that some have thought they could find in Novatian's extant works of a voluntary exile during the persecutions of Gallus, Volusian, or Valerian.[27] Socrates, the fifth-century historian, claims that Novatian suffered martyrdom: "He himself indeed afterwards suffered martyrdom in the reign of Valerian, during the persecution which was then raised against the Christians."[28] We must bear in mind, however, that Socrates was sympathetic to the Novatianists and the accuracy of his statement is suspect. The Egyptian Novatianists of the sixth century possessed, according to the testimony of Eulogius (d. 607), bishop of Alexandria, acts of the martyrdom of Novatian, but these Photius dismisses as completely worthless.[29] We must note, observes H. Valesius, that in these acts of martyrdom Novatian is not represented as suffering martyrdom, but simply as being a "confessor."[30] The Novatianist deacon, Sympronian, claimed that Cyprian, the first African bishop to be martyred, in one of his letters was alluding to Novatian when he wrote: "My adversary preceded me."[31] Pacian, bishop of Barcelona, challenged the statement.[32] In the martyrology falsely attributed to St. Jerome a Novatian—no title or rank is given and the spelling varies—is listed as a martyr both at Cordova, Spain (June

25 Cyprian, *Ep.* 55.26 (CSEL 3.2.644; FC 51.151).
26 Eusebius, *Hist. eccl.* 6.42 (FC 29.78-79).
27 *Novatiani opera* . . . (CCL 4) xi.
28 Socrates, *Hist. eccl.* 4.28 (PG 67.540A).
29 Photius, *Bibl.* Cod. 182, 208 (Henry, 2.194, 3.105); Vogt, *op. cit.*, 24.
30 H. Valesius, *Annotationes Socratis Hist. eccl.* 96 (PG 67.539 [from the original edition of 1668]); excerpts of Eulogius' treatise against the Novatianists are found in Photius, *Bibl.* Cod. 182, 208, 280 (PG 103.533C, 677C; 104.353: Henry, 2.192, 3.105 [Cod. 280 passage not yet published in Henry]).
31 Pacian, *Ep. ad Sympronianum* 2.7 (PL 13.1062C).
32 *Ibid.*

27) and at Rome (June 29).[33] On April 1, 1932, a tomb was uncovered in a recently discovered cemetery near St. Lawrence in Rome with the inscription:

NOVATIANO BEATISSIMO MARTYRI
GAUDENTIUS DIAC[ONUS]
FEC[IT]

that is, "To Novatian, the most blessed martyr, the deacon Gaudentius made . . .." Whether this inscription refers to Novatian the antipope or to some other person is highly controversial.[34]

Novatian was a prolific writer. He was the first Roman theologian to write in Latin and his works are intimately linked with the beginnings of Latin Christian literature at Rome. According to Jerome, Novatian wrote: *"De pascha (The Passover), De sabbato (The Sabbath), De circumcisione (Circumcision), De sacerdote (The Priesthood), De oratione (Prayer), De cibis Iudaicis (Jewish Foods), De instantia (Zeal), De Attalo (Attalus),* and many other works, especially a great volume *De trinitate (The Trinity)."*[35] Of the works here named, only *The Trinity* and *Jewish Foods* are extant, surviving among the works of Tertullian. In his *Jewish Foods* Novatian himself alludes to two of the works mentioned by Jerome: "I have fully shown in two former letters what is the true circumcision and what the true Sabbath."[36] Jerome does not include *The Spectacles* and *In Praise of Purity* in his enumeration of Novatian's works. This can easily be explained. In 392, when Jerome was drawing up the enumeration given in his *Illustrious Men,* "many other works" of Novatian were in circulation which Jerome had not yet in his posses-

33 *Martyrologium Hieronymianum,* ed. H. Quentin (with commentary by H. Delehaye), *Acta sanctorum Nov.* 2.2 (1931) 337 (with n. 31, p. 338; Delehaye does not reject the possibility that ours is the Novatian intended), 342 (with n. 20, p. 343). See also the earlier edition (I. B. de Rossi and L. Duchesne), *Acta sanct. Nov.* 2.1 (1894) [83], [84].
34 See A. P. Frutaz, "Novaziano, Cimitero detto di," EC 8 (1952) 1974-76 (1975, photo of the inscription), and esp. Vogt, *Coetus Sanctorum* 24-27, 286-87.
35 *De vir. ill.* 70 (PL 23.681; ed. Richardson p. 39; see above n. 3).
36 *De cibis Iudaicis* 1.6.

sion. Novatian's *Spectacles* and *In Praise of Purity* survived among
the works of Cyprian. Jerome mentions elsewhere a collection of
letters written by Novatian (*epistolas Novatiani*),[37] and Cyprian
frequently speaks of letters written by Novatian.[38] We also have the
testimony of Socrates that Novatian "wrote to all the churches
everywhere."[39] However, as we have already mentioned, only three
of Novatian's letters survived, preserved among the letters of
Cyprian. Thus, no works of Novatian have come down to us under
his own name. "It would seem," observes E. J. Goodspeed, "that the
ancients found so much value in them that they could not resist
copying them but could not bring themselves to credit them to the
notorious Roman schismatic."[40]

   The schismatic Church founded by Novatian spread to every sector
of the Christian world. His theory of a Messianic Church, heroic and in
conflict with the world, was virtually a renewal of the conflict between Hippolytus and Callistus.[41] Then, too, many of Novatian's
rigorist ideas had come to him from his reading of Tertullian. Towards the latter part of his life, Tertullian the Montanist came to
regard the body of the faithful as a select group.[42] The Church of
the Spirit and the Church of the bishops were placed in opposition.[43] On the other hand there was the theory of the Church held
by the great bishops of the ancient Church: the Church was for all
men; there was a place for an élite of spiritually minded people
(prophets, martyrs, confessors, and virgins) but there was also room
for a multitude of ordinary Christians. This attitude of the early
bishops in no way undermined the integrity of the Gospel; it was the
traditional attitude of the Church.[44]

---

37 *Ep.* 10.3 (tr. by C. C. Mierow, ACW 33.51; cf. the note of T. C. Lawler,
   ibid. 203).
38 Cf. *Epp.* 44.1; 45.2; 55.1, 5 (CSEL 3.2.597 etc.; FC 51.112 etc.).
39 Socrates, *Hist. eccl.* 4.28 (PG 67.538B).
40 E.J. Goodspeed, *A History of Early Christian Literature* (Chicago 1966)
   180.
41 Daniélou-Marrou, *The Christian Centuries* 198-99.
42 *De pudicitia* 21.17 (CCL 2.1328; tr. by W. Le Saint, ACW 28.122).
43 Quasten, *Patrology* 2.331.
44 Daniélou-Marrou, *The Christian Centuries* 196-97, 199.

The Novatianist churches continued to thrive side by side with the orthodox churches up to the fifth century in the West and up to the eighth century in the East, especially in Asia Minor. In the West, Novatianist communities with their own bishops spread from Rome and Africa as far as Spain. Innocent I (401-17) closed some of their churches; Celestine I (422-32) expelled them from Rome. In the fifth century, Donatus of Salasia, a Novatianist bishop, returned with his entire community to the Church.[45] In the East, many of the cities of Phrygia, former stronghold of the Montanists, had Novatianist bishops. In Syria the Novatianists lasted for several centuries. The historian Socrates, though not a Novatianist, shows a remarkable interest in the Novatianist church and admiration for Novatianist personalities and principles. He treats of Novatianist origins[46] and gives an account of the Novatianist bishops of Constantinople.[47] Ascesius, the Novatianist bishop of Constantinople, was invited by the emperor to attend the Council of Nicaea.[48] The Novatianists were tolerated by the Catholic party of the *homoousios* formula. The last of their communities survived till the end of the seventh century.

As is suggested in the separate introductions to the several works of Novatian, it is, in the last analysis, G. F. Dierck's just published edition of Novatian[49] that forms the basis of this translation. Material he includes in square brackets is simply ignored in this translation (the square brackets that appear in the translation enclose explanations that seemed essential for the English reader). What Diercks has added to the text found in the manuscripts, enclos-

---

45 Leo I, *Ep.* 12 (PL 54.653; FC 34.54).
46 Socrates, *Hist. eccl.* 4.28 (PG 76.538-41).
47 Socrates, *op. cit.* 1.10; 5.21; 6.21, 22; 7.11, 12, 17, 46 (PG 67. 99B, 622-26, 726-30, 757-60, 771-74, 837-40).
48 Socrates, *op. cit.* 1.10 (PG 67.99B).
49 The first to publish together, in the original, and under their author's name all the works known to be Novatian's. Similarly the present volume, planned before the appearance of Dierck's edition, is the first to assemble translations of those same works under Novatian's name. All of them appear in R. E. Wallis's English version, but there only *The Trinity, Jewish Foods,* and our Letter 1 are assigned to Novatian.

ing it in angle brackets, <>, has regularly been taken into account in the translation and here too set between angle brackets.

So far as was feasible, the Scriptural quotations found in Novatian's text are represented by the English of *The New American Bible* (1970) or, in some cases, of one or another of the successive editions in which the components of this translation, sponsored by the Bishops' Committee of the Confraternity of Christian Doctrine, made their first appearances.[50]

*   *   *

My grateful thanks are extended to Dr. Johannes Quasten, an incomparable teacher, whose enthusiasm for Novatian has served as a constant incentive to me, and to Dr. G. F. Diercks for sending me the proofs of his critical edition.

RUSSELL J. DESIMONE, O.S.A.

---

50 Especially the *New Catholic Edition of the Holy Bible* (1954).

THE TRINITY

INTRODUCTION

HE PREEMINENCE IN ROMAN LATIN THEOLOGY of Novatian's work *The Trinity* (*De Trinitate*) may be judged from the relevant patristic writing that preceded it. There had been Minucius Felix, who wrote at Rome and in Latin his dialogue, the *Octavius,* but the aim and scope of this single surviving work do not establish its author as a theologian. The Roman theologian Hippolytus wrote in Greek. Greek may also have been the original language of the Muratorian Fragment, whose eighty-five surviving lines of unschooled Latin do no more than enumerate and briefly discuss the writings of the New Testament—a text highly important for biblical studies but one that cannot assure to its unknown author the title of theologian. The great Tertullian, though he spent some years at Rome, was born in Carthage and belongs to the African Latin church. In the two letters in Latin surviving from the pen of Pope Cornelius, whom Novatian opposed, we do not sense a theologian's hand or purpose. In *The Trinity,* in fact, Novatian stands indeed virtually unchallenged in Roman Latin theology.[1]

Harnack is eloquent in his evaluation of *The Trinity*:

> This first great Latin work that appeared in Rome is highly important. In regard to completeness, extent of Biblical proofs, and perhaps also its influence on succeeding times, it may in many respects be compared with Origen's *First Principles* .... He thereby created for the West a dogmatic *vademecum,* which from its copious and well-selected quotations from Scripture, must have been of extraordinary service.[2]

1 R. DeSimone, *The Treatise of Novatian the Roman Presbyter on the Trinity: A Study of the Text and the Doctrine* (Studia Ephemeridis "Augustinianum" 4; Rome 1970) 44.

2 A. Harnack, *History of Dogma* (tr. by N. Buchanan, Boston 1907) 2.313-15.

Likewise noteworthy is the recent judgement of W.A. Jurgens: "In the development of Trinitarian Theology, . . . [Novatian] was at least a hundred years ahead of his contemporaries."[3]

The Trinity was written before the year 250. The following considerations justify such a conclusion: (1) The work does not contain any reference to the Decian persecution (250-51). (2) It shows no trace of Novatian's heresy regarding the power of the keys. If Novatian had written it after his break with the church (April 251), he would have undoubtedly used it to defend his position. (3) There are two references to Sabellius and his heresy (ch. 12); therefore, it was probably written between 240 and 250.

Novatian wrote *The Trinity* as a commentary on the Rule of Faith.[4] For Novatian the Rule of Faith is "the tradition and teaching of Christ."[5] In the opening chapters (1-8) of his treatise, he paints a magnificent picture of the majesty and transcendence of "God the Father and almighty Lord" who is, however, immediately and directly associated with His work: "The indefatigable providence of God embraces even the least things." Against the Gnostics, Novatian insists that "God the Father is the Creator of all things" (ch. 1). Some of the Christian writers were less affirmative than Novatian regarding the spirituality (absolute immateriality) of God.[6]

Novatian devotes the whole of chapters 12-28 to the unrelenting demonstration of the divinity of Christ.[7] His demonstration can be conveniently divided, in general, as follows: (1) scriptural proofs (chs. 12-13, 17-22); (2) theological proofs (chs. 14-16); (3) proofs drawn from the adversaries (chs. 23-28). Novatian rendered the Church of his time a great service by defending her doctrine against

---

3 W.A. Jurgens, *The Faith of the Early Fathers* (Collegeville, Minn., 1970) 247.

4 G. Kretschmar, *Studien zur frühchristlichen Trinitätstheologie* (Tübingen 1956) 128; cf. M. E. Williams, art. "Rule of Faith," NCE 12.706-7.

5 *De cib. Iud.* 1 and 7; cf. Y. M. J. Congar, *Tradition and Traditions* (New York 1967) 27.

6 M. Spanneut, *Le stoïcisme des pères de l'Église* (Paris 1957) 289-91; M. Kreibel, *Studien zur älteren Entwicklung der abendländischen Trinitätslehre bei Tertullian und Novatian* (diss., Ohlau-Marburg 1932) 19-20; W. Le Saint, "Tertullian," NCE 13.1022. See, however, J. Moingt, *Théologie trinitaire de Tertullien* (Paris 1966) 299-338.

7 See R. DeSimone, "Christ the True God and True Man according to Novatian, 'De Trinitate,' " *Augustinianum* 10 (1970) 62-67.

the errors of Docetism, Adoptianism, and Modalism. Novatian's
second series of positive proofs (chs. 17-22) for the divinity of
Christ are drawn chiefly (with the exception of chs. 21 and 22) from
the theophanies of the Old Testament. These serve to demonstrate
the independent personality and divinity of the Son.[8]

Although Novatian's theological language is closely dependent on
that of Tertullian,[9] his theological terminology and precise dogmatic
formulae evidence a marked progress,[10] enabling the West to meet
the Greeks on equal terms in the christological controversy.[11] One
must await the middle of the third century to witness the
appearance of the Western equivalent of the Greek *sarkōtheís* (incarnate), which appears for the first time in Novatian (ch. 24.7
incarnatus).[12]

When Novatian speaks of the *persona Christi* it is always in a Trinitarian sense because he wants to stress the distinction of Father and
Son. He expresses the union of the two substances in Christ with the
formula *una concordia* (chs. 13.3, 21.8, 23.7, 24.11), not *una persona*.[13] *Una persona* has a strict Christological meaning only at the
beginning of the fifth century in the writings of Jerome and
Augustine (411 A.D.).[14] Novatian, however, strengthened the ter-
minological link between Christology and Trinitarian doctrine.[15] In
his polemics with the Adoptianists, the Docetists, and the Modalists,
Novatian places the "Son of God" and the "Son of Man" in sharp
contrast (ch.13); he does not fail, however, to stress the "Word-

8 *Ibid.* 88-108; G. Aeby, *Les missions divines de Saint Justin à Origène*
(Fribourg 1958) 103-15; cf. Moingt, *op. cit.* 255-62.

9 R. Braun, *"Deus Christianorum": Recherches sur le vocabulaire doctrinal
de Tertullien* (Paris 1962) 167 n. 1.

10 Mohrmann, in *Vigiliae Christianae* 3 (1949) 168 (*Etudes . . . 3.*111).

11 Quasten, *Patrology* 2.232-33.

12 Braun, *op. cit.* 302

13 R. Cantalamessa, *La Cristologia di Tertulliano* (Fribourg 1962) 169.

14 See Mohrmann's book review of T. J. van Bavel, *Recherches sur la Chris-
tologie de saint Augustin* (Fribourg 1954) in *Vigiliae Christianae* 10 (1956)
59.

15 R. Favre, "La Communication des idiomes dans l'ancienne tradition
latine," *Bulletin de littérature ecclésiastique* 37 (1936) 130-45; A.
Grillmeier, *Christ in Christian Tradition* (New York 1965) 157.

flesh" framework. Novatian, as A. Grillmeier[16] points out, finds no difficulty in fitting together two frameworks of christological thought (the old Roman Logos-*sarx* Christology put forward by Hippolytus and growing traces of the *Verbum-homo* framework of later Latin theology) when he states:

> And how is He the firstborn of all creatures, if not by virtue of His being that divine Word (*divinum Verbum illud*) that is before every creature? Therefore, the firstborn of all creatures is made flesh (*caro fit*) and dwells among us—that is, He assumes this humanity (*hunc hominem*) which is after all creation—and thus, with it and in it, dwells among us, so that neither is humanity taken away from Christ nor is divinity denied Him (ch. 21.6).

Novatian speaks of *concretio, permixtio, connexio, confibulatio* of the two substances in Christ (ch. 11.1, 24.8-11, 25.3 and 5). He conceives this union of the two substances in Christ according to the Stoic *krâsis di' hólōn* or total compenetration of the descending "Spirit" (=Logos) and the assumed Son of man:[17]

> Primarily, however, the Son of God is the Word of God Incarnate *(Verbum dei incarnatum)* . . . This is the genuine Son of God, who is of God Himself. Inasmuch as He assumes that *holy thing* and joins to Himself the Son of Man, He not only seizes Him and draws Him over to Himself but also bestows upon Him and makes Him by His connection (*connexione*) and associated permixtion (*permixtione*) the Son of God, which He was not by nature. Thus, the pre-eminence of that name: *Son of God* resides in the Spirit of the Lord who descended and came (*in spiritu sit domini qui descendit*); whereas the sequela of that name is to be found in the Son of God and Man. In consequence of such a union this son Man rightly became the Son of God, although He is not primarily the Son of God (ch. 24.7-8).

Novatian clearly affirms the pre-temporal Sonship of the Word:

> Since He is begotten of the Father, He is always in the Father. I say "always," however, in such a manner, not to prove that He is

16 Grillmeier, *op. cit.* 158-59.
17 *Ibid.* 157; Cantalamessa, *op. cit.* 147-8.

unborn, but born. Now, He who is before all time, must be said to have been always in the Father; for no time can be attributed to Him who is before time. He is always in the Father, lest the Father be not always the Father (ch. 31.3).

Novatian has arrived at a rather pure concept of the generation of the Word. Father and Son are correlative notions. Novatian distinguishes the generation of the Word from His procession as Lord and Creator. He is cautiously making his way toward a synthesis between the heritage of the Apologists and the data provided by Tertullian and Hippolytus. He clings to the subordinationism of the former, that is, the procession linked to creation. From the latter, he takes the distinction between the first eternal generation and a second one linked to time. He succeeded, better than they did, in disengaging the eternal generation from every tie to creation and clearly demonstrated that the relation between Father and Son is *eternal and necessary.* Thus the generation of the Son is not linked to creation and the mystery of man's salvation. This is a theological breakthrough because Novatian succeeded, as no one before him had, in setting free the inner life of God from all consideration of time.[18]

Although all that he says presupposes it, Novatian's primary purpose is not to prove the personal existence of the Holy Spirit (chs. 16.2-3; 29). Novatian does not expressly give the Holy Spirit the name of God. Novatian's primary objective is to refute the Gnostics, to demonstrate that it is the same Spirit who had been given to the apostles, and to expound the work of the Holy Spirit in the formation of the Church and the sanctification of souls. The Gnostics maintained that the Holy Spirit (whatever was the sense they attached to the name) was the principle of spiritual men or of the "pneumatics". Novatian expounds the sanctifying power of the Holy Spirit in a more complete and explicit manner than his predecessors, Irenaeus, Hippolytus, and Tertullian. Novatian surpassed Tertullian who was chiefly concerned with the Paraclete and the revelations of the

18 J. N. D. Kelly, *Early Christian Doctrines* (2nd ed., New York 1960) 125-26; G. Sloyan, *The Three Persons in One God* (Englewood Cliffs, N. J., 1964) 45-46; Aeby, *op. cit.* (n. 8) 107-11.

"new prophecy", and had little time for the interior life of the
Christian, lived in the grace of the Holy Spirit. Novatian brought this
Pauline doctrine to the forefront.[19] We find in Novatian's work a
serious effort to gather together the Scriptural texts pertaining to
the action of the Holy Spirit. To Novatian the Holy Spirit is not a
mere creature, as M. Simonetti[20] maintains, but a Divine Person.[21]
Furthermore, I cannot endorse Simonetti's conclusion that Novatian
"never gives any indication that he ever had a Trinitarian concept of
the divinity." [22] Much of Novatian's teaching on the Holy Spirit was
taken over by Gregory (Gregorius Iliberritanus), bishop of Elvira
near Granada, who died sometime after the year 392.[23]

In the closing chapters of his work, Novatian eloquently exclaims:
"Indeed the Lord is crucified, as it were, between two thieves, just as
He was once crucified; and so He is exposed on either side to the
impious revilings of the heretics" (ch. 30.6). Novatian is referring to
the Modalists and the Adoptianists. He demonstrates that the two
fundamental truths that the heretics considered irreconcilable, namely, the unity of God and the divinity of Christ, are completely
compatible.

In the final chapter, Novatian does not teach the false theory, final
reabsorption of the Son into the Father, which was attributed to
Marcellus of Ancyra. Novatian merely wants to say: "The Son is
indeed shown to be God, since it is clear that the divinity has been
handed over and granted to Him. Nevertheless, the Father proves to
be one God" (ch. 31.21).[24]

19 E. Evans, Q. S. Fl. Tertullianus. Treatise against Praxeas (London 1948) 28.
20 M. Simonetti, "Alcune osservazioni sul De Trinitate di Novaziano," Studi
     in onore di Angelo Monteverdi 2 (Modena 1959) 779.
21 R. DeSimone, "The Holy Spirit according to Novatian 'De Trinitate,' "
     Augustinianum 10 (1970) 376ff. Cf. H. Weyer, Novatianus: De Trini-
     tate . . . (Düsseldorf 1962) 27, 182 n. 102. Cf. Vogt, op. cit. 87: "It
     should not thereby be said that the Spirit is not a Person. On the contrary,
     the many quite personal activities that are ascribed to Him appear to point
     absolutely to His personality."
22 Simonetti, op. cit. 783. For my position, see DeSimone, "The Holy Spirit, '
     381-82; cf. Moingt, op. cit. (n. 6) 53-86.
23 See Tractatus Origenis 20.54-61, 89-150 (ed. V. Bulhart, CCL 69.143-46).
24 Weyer, op. cit. 204-6.

In conclusion, we must bear in mind that Novatian is energetically defending against the Gnostics, Docetists, Adoptianists, and Sabellianists. He is not concerned with irrelevant, subtle questions. He upholds the real human nature and divinity of Christ. He strives to place in bold relief the posteriority of the Son, insofar as His origin is concerned, so that he can better defend the personal distinction of the Father and the Son. He has been charged with subordinationism. Novatian, however, did not make use of explicit formulas to formally defend subordinationism.

The present translation is based on the critical texts of W. Y. Fausset (Cambridge 1909) and H. Weyer (Düsseldorf 1962). Through the kindness of G. F. Diercks I was able to use the proof sheets of his own critical edition: *Novatiani opera . . .* in *Corpus Christianorum,* Series Latin 4 (Turnhout 1972). His excellent emendations of the above editions have been incorporated in the present translation.

SELECT BIBLIOGRAPHY

Texts:

Diercks, G. F. *Novatiani Opera* . . . (CCL 4; Turnhout 1972) 1-78.
Fausset, W. Y. *Novatiani Romanae urbis presbyteri De Trinitate liber* (Cambridge Patristic Texts; Cambridge 1909).
Migne, J.-P. *Patrologia Latina* 3 (Paris 1886) 861-970.
Weyer, H. *Novatianus De Trinitate Uber den dreifaltigen Gott;* with German translation (Testimonia 2; Düsseldorf 1962).

Translations:

Moore, H. *The Treatise of Novatian on the Trinity* (Society for Promoting Christian Knowledge, London 1919).
Wallis, R. E. in *The Ante-Nicene Fathers* 5 (New York 1926) 611-44; *Ante-Nicene Christian Library* 13 (Edinburgh 1880) 293-381.

Secondary Sources:

D'Alès, A. *Novatien: Étude sur la théologie romaine au milieu du IIIe siècle* (Paris 1925).
DeSimone, R. *The Treatise of Novatian the Roman Presbyter on the Trinity: A Study of the Text and the Doctrine* (Studia Ephemeridis "Augustinianum" 4, Rome 1970).
– – – – –, "Christ the True God and True Man according to Novatian 'De Trinitate'," *Augustinianum* 10 (1970) 42-117.
– – – – –, "The Holy Spirit according to Novatian 'De Trinitate'," *ibid.* 360-87.
Keilbach, G. "Divinitas Filii eiusque Patri subordinatio in Novatiani libro de Trinitate," *Bogoslovska Smotra* 21 (1933) 193-224.
Kriebel, M. *Studien zur älteren Entwicklung der abendländischen Trinitätslehre bei Tertullian und Novatian* (diss., Marburg 1932).
Loi, V. "La Latinità cristiana nel *De Trinitate* di Novaziano," *Rivista di cultura classica e medioevale* 12 (1971) 1-42.
Pelikan, J. *The Christian Tradition: A History of the Development of Doctrine* 1 (*The Emergence of the Catholic Tradition* [*100-600*]) (Chicago - London 1971).
Quasten, J. *Patrology* 2 (Westminster, Md. 1953) 217-19, 226-33.
Simonetti, M. "Alcune osservazioni sul De Trinitate di Novaziano," *Studi in onore di Angelo Monteverdi* 2 (Modena 1959) 771-83.

CONTENTS

THE TRINITY

Chapter 1

HE RULE OF TRUTH[1] requires that we believe, first in God the Father and almighty Lord, the most perfect Creator of all things. He suspended the heavens above in their lofty height,[2] made firm the earth with the heavy mass under it, poured forth the freely flowing water of the seas;[3] and He arranged all these, in full abundance and order, with appropriate and suitable appurtenances.[4] (2) In the firmament of heaven He summoned forth the light of the rising sun. He filled the candescent sphere of the moon with its monthly waxings to relieve the darkness.[5] He also illuminated the rays of the stars with varying flashes of twinkling light. He willed that all these things in their lawfully regulated orbits[6] encircle the entire earth's surface to form days, months, years, seasons, signs, and other things useful for mankind. (3) On earth He lifted up the highest mountains to a peak, threw down the valleys into the lowlands, leveled the plains, and created the different kinds of animals for the various needs of man. (4) He also hardened the sturdy trees of the forests to serve man's needs, brought forth the fruits of the earth for food, opened the

---

1 The original title of the treatise is unknown. The correct title seems to have been *De regula veritatis (The Rule of Truth)* or *De regula fidei (The Rule of Faith)*. Novatian makes it clear that his purpose in writing was "to explain briefly the Rule of Faith" (ch. 21). He never uses the word "Trinity." The Trinitarian controversies which took place between the Councils of Nicaea and Constantinople probably inspired an amanuensis to alter the original title.

2 Cf. Gen. 1.6.

3 Cf. Gen. 1.9-10.

4 Cf. Gen. 1.14-18; 1 Cor. 15.41. Novatian's admiration of creation betrays Stoic influence.

5 Cf. Tertullian, *Adversus Hermogenem* 29; Vergil, *Aeneid* 6.270.

6 Cf. Theophilus of Antioch, *Ad Autolycum* 1.4,6; Tertullian, *Adv. Marcionem* 2.3.

mouths of springs, and poured them into the flowing rivers.[7] (5) After these things, lest He should have failed to provide our eyes with beautiful objects, He clothed all things with the various colors of flowers to delight all those who look upon them. (6) Although the sea was wonderful both in its extent and for its usefulness, yet in it also He fashioned many kinds of living creatures, both small and large,[8] which show the intelligence of the Creator by the variety of His creation. (7) Not content with all this, lest the rushing and the flowing of the waters occupy territory not its own with loss to its human possessor, He enclosed its limits with shores, so that when the roaring waves and the foaming surge would come forth from the sea's bosom, they would return into themselves and would not pass beyond the limits allowed them.[9] They would obey their prescribed laws, in order that man would more readily keep God's laws, seeing that even the elements themselves obey them.

(8) After all these things had been accomplished, He placed man at the head of the world--man made to the image of God,[10] endowed with intelligence, discernment, and prudence so that he could imitate God. Although the primordial elements of his body were earthly, nevertheless the substance was infused by a heavenly and divine breath.[11] (9) When God gave him all these things for his service, He willed that man alone should be free.[12] Nevertheless, lest man's unrestrained freedom prove dangerous, God imposed a command in which He stated that indeed evil was not in the fruit of the tree,[13] but warned that evil would follow if, in the use of his free will, man disregarded the command laid down.[14] (10) On the one hand, man ought to be free lest the image of God serve in unbecoming manner.

7 Cf. Ps. 103(104).10.
8 Cf. Ps. 103(104).25.
9 Cf. Ps. 103(104).9.
10 Cf. Gen. 1.26-27.
11 Cf. Gen. 2.7.
12 Cf. Gen. 1.28.
13 Cf. Gen. 2.17; Theophilus of Antioch, *Ad Autol.* 2.25.
14 Cf. Plato, *The Republic* 10.617E: "The blame is his who chooses: God is blameless," quoted by Justin Martyr, *Apology* 1.44 (tr. by T. B. Falls, FC 6.81). Cf. also Tertullian, *Adv. Marc.* 2.4, 6, 7, and Theophilus, *Ad Autol.* 2.27.

On the other hand, a law had to be imposed that unrestrained liberty might not break forth even to contempt for its Giver. Hence, man might receive either merited rewards or due punishments as the result of his actions, recognizing these actions as his own doings, because it was in his power to act, through the movement of his mind in the one or the other direction.[15] (11) Whence, indeed, hated mortality comes back upon him.[16] He could have avoided mortality by obedience, but he subjected himself to it by his headlong and perverse determination to be God.[17] (12) Nevertheless, God mercifully mitigated his punishment by cursing not so much man as his labors on earth.[18] The fact that God searches for him does not proceed from any ignorance on the part of God[19] but it manifests man's hope of a future discovery and salvation in Christ.[20] Furthermore, that man was prevented from touching the wood of the tree of life[21] did not spring from the malicious ill-will of envy but from a fear that man, living forever, would always bear about with him for his punishment an abiding guilt,[22] had not Christ previously pardoned his sins.

(13) In the higher regions—those above the very firmament itself, which at present are beyond our sight—He previously called the angels into being, arranged the spiritual powers, set over them the Thrones and Powers, created many other measureless spaces of heavens and mysterious works without limit. Therefore, even this measureless universe seems to be the latest of God's material creations rather than His only work. (14) Even the regions that lie beneath the earth are not without their ruling powers duly appointed and set out. For there is a place to which are taken the souls of the just and the unjust, already aware of the sentence awaiting them

15 Cf. 2 Cor. 5.10.
16 Cf. Wisd. 2.24 (?). Novatian means envy on the part of God; he is combating heresy (cf. Theophilus, *Ad Autol.* 2.25).
17 Cf. Gen. 3.5.
18 Cf. Gen. 3.17.
19 Cf. Gen. 3.9; Luke 19.10; Theophilus, *Ad Autol.* 2.26; Tertullian, *Adv. Marc.* 2.25.
20 Cf. Rom. 8.19-21.
21 Cf. Gen. 2.17.
22 Cf. Irenaeus, *Adv. haereses* 3.23.6; Theophilus, *Ad Autol.* 2.26.

at the future judgment. We see, therefore, that the vast works of God, exuberant on all sides, are not shut up within the confines of this world spacious to the utmost as we have said; but we can also contemplate them beneath both the depths and the heights of the world itself. Thus, after having considered the greatness of His works, we can fittingly admire the Maker of such a mighty mass.[23]

Chapter 2

Over all these things is God Himself, who contains all things and who leaves nothing devoid of Himself; He has left no room for a superior god[1] as some think. Since He Himself has enclosed all things in the bosom of His perfect greatness and power, He is always intent on His own work and pervades all things, moves all things, gives life to all things, and observes all things.[2] He binds together the discordant materials of all the elements into such harmony[3] that out of these dissimilar elements, there exists a unique world so compacted by this consolidated harmony that no force can dissolve it, save when He alone who created it orders it to be dissolved in order to grant us greater blessings.[4] (2) We read that He contains all things;[5] therefore nothing could have existed outside of Him. For indeed He who has no beginning whatsoever, must necessarily experience no end, unless—far be the thought from us—He began to exist at a certain time and is therefore not above all things. But if He began to exist after something else, He would be inferior to that previously existing thing; hence He would be found to be of lesser power, since designated as subsequent even in time itself. (3) For this reason, therefore, He is always infinite because there is nothing greater than

23 Cf. Vergil, *Aen.* 1.33.

1 That is, the God of Marcion; cf. Tertullian, *Adv. Marc.* 1.15.
2 Novatian describes here the cosmic function of God the Creator and Organizer of the world.
3 Cf. Ovid, *Metamorphoses* 1.25. We have here the theory of *"contraires complémentaires"* which was also attributed in general to the Stoics (Spanneut, *op. cit.* [Intr. to *The Trinity* n. 5] 379, 412-13).
4 Cf. 2 Peter 3.10-12; Rev. 21.1.
5 Cf. Wisd. 1.7 (?); Isa. 40.22 (?).

He, ever eternal, because nothing is more ancient than He. In fact, that which is without a beginning can be preceded by nothing, because it lacks time. Therefore He is immortal, for He does not pass away to a consummate end. And since whatever is without a beginning is without a law, He excludes the restrictions of time because He feels Himself a debtor to no one.

(4) Concerning Him, therefore, and concerning those things which are of Him and in Him, the mind of man cannot fittingly conceive what they are, how great they are, and of what their nature; nor has human eloquence the power to express His greatness. (5) For all eloquence is certainly dumb and every mind is inadequate to conceive and to utter His greatness.[6] In fact, He is greater than the mind itself, so that His greatness is inconceivable; for if He could be conceived, He would be less than the human mind which could conceive Him. He is also greater than all speech, so that He cannot be expressed; for if He could be expressed, He would be less than human speech, which through expressing Him would then comprehend and contain Him. (6) Whatever can be thought about Him is less than He; whatever can be uttered about Him will be less than He when compared with Him. When we are silent we can experience Him to some extent, but we cannot express Him in words as He really is. (7) If, for instance, you should speak of Him as light,[7] you would be speaking of a created thing of His, not of Him, you would not express what He is. If you should speak of Him as power, you would be speaking of and bringing out His might rather than Himself. If you should speak of Him as majesty, you would be describing His honor rather than Him. (8) But why am I making a protracted affair of this matter by running through His attributes one by one? Once and for all I will sum up everything: whatever you might affirm about Him would be expressing some possession or power of His rather than God Himself. (9) For what can you fittingly say or think about Him who is above all speech and thought? There is only

6 Novatian's description of God's transcendental attributes reveals Neoplatonic and Platonic influence.
7 Cf. Theophilus, *Ad Autol.* 1.3.

one thing that can fittingly be said or thought about Him who is above all speech and thought: namely, that—within our power, our grasp, our understanding—there is only one way in which we may mentally conceive what God is—viz., by realizing that He is that Being of whose nature and greatness there is no possible understanding, nor even any possibility of thinking.[8] (10) If the keen sight of our eyes grows dim by looking at the sun so that their gaze, overpowered by the bright rays that meet it, cannot look at the orb itself, our mental vision undergoes this very same thing in its every thought of God. The more it endeavors to contemplate God, the more is it blinded by the light of its own thought. (11) In fact, what (to repeat once more) can you worthily say about Him, who is more sublime than all sublimity, loftier than all loftiness, more profound than all profundity, brighter than all light, more brilliant than all brilliance, more splendid than all splendor, mightier than all might, more powerful than all power, more beautiful than all beauty, truer than all truth, stronger than all strength, greater than all majesty, more potent than all potency, richer than all riches, and more prudent than all prudence, and kinder than all kindness, better than all goodness, more just than all justice, more clement than all clemency? (12) Every kind of virtue must of necessity be less than He who is the God and Author of them all, so that it can really be said that God is that which is of such a nature that nothing can be compared to him. For He is above everything that can be said of Him. He is, so to speak, an intelligent Being who without any beginning or ending in time engenders and fills all things and governs, for the good of all, with supreme and perfect reason, the causes of things naturally linked together.

Chapter 3

We acknowledge, therefore, and know that He is God, the Creator[1] of all things; their Lord, because of His power; their

8 It almost sounds like Plotinus discussing God's ineffable immensity.

1 Cf. Vergil, *Aen.* 8.313.

Author, because of creation. "He, " I say, "spoke and all things were made ; He commanded, and all things came forth."[2] Of Him it is written: "You have made all things in wisdom."[3] Moses says of Him: "God is in heaven above and on earth below,"[4] and according to Isaiah, "He has measured the heavens with a span, the earth with the width of the fist;[5] who looks upon the earth and makes it tremble;[6] who holds the orb of the earth and those who live on it as if they were locusts;[7] who weighed the mountains on scales and the groves on a balance,[8] by the exact precision of the divine plan. And He laid out this weight of the earth's mass with precise equipoise, lest the huge ill-balanced mass should easily fall to ruin, if it were not balanced with proportionate weights.[9] It is He who says through the prophet: "I am God, and there is none beside Me."[10] He says by means of the same prophet: "I will not give My majesty to another,"[11] so that He might exclude all heathens and heretics with their images, proving that he is not God who is made by the hand of an artificer;[12] nor is he God whom heretical ingenuity,[13] has devised. For he is not God whose existence requires an artificer. (3) Again, He says through the prophet: "Heaven is My throne, earth the footstool under My feet: what sort of home will you build for Me, or what is the place of My rest?"[14]—this to make it clear that since the world cannot contain Him, much less can a temple enclose Him. God says these things for our instruction, not to boast of Himself. Nor does He seek from us glory for His own greatness; rather, as a Father, He

2 Ps. 148.5.
3 Ps. 103(104).24.
4 Deut. 4.39.
5 Isa. 40.12.
6 Ps. 103(104).32.
7 Isa. 40.22.
8 Isa. 40.12.
9 Ps. 103(104).5.
10 Isa. 45.21-22; cf. 18.
11 Isa. 42.8; 48.11.
12 Hosea 8.6; Acts 19.26.
13 Tertullian (De praescriptione haereticorum 40) also places idolaters and heretics in the same category.
14 Isa. 66.1.

desires to bestow on us God-fearing wisdom. (4) He desires, moreover,
to attract our minds, so cruel, so proud, and so obstinate in their
rude ferocity, to gentleness;[15] hence He says: "And upon whom
shall My spirit rest but upon him who is humble and peaceful, and
trembles at my words?"[16] Thus man may know, to some extent,
how great God is, while he learns to fear Him through the spirit
given to him. (5) Ever desiring to become more completely known
to us and to incite our minds to His worship, He said: "I am the
Lord who made the light and created the darkness,"[17] that we may
not think that a certain "nature"—I know not what—was the artificer[18]
of those alternations whereby the nights and days are regulated; but
rather, and with greater truth, we may acknowledge God as their
Creator. (6) Since we cannot see Him with the sight of our eyes, we
learn to know Him from the greatness, the power, and the majesty
of His works. "For since the creation of the world," says the
Apostle, "His invisible attributes are clearly seen—His everlasting
power also and divinity—being understood through the things that
are made.[19] Thus the human mind, learning to know the hidden
things from those which are manifest, may consider in spirit the
greatness of the Maker from the greatness of His works which it sees
with the eyes of the mind.[20] (7) The same Apostle says of Him: "To
the King of the ages, who is immortal, invisible, the one only God,
be honor and glory."[21] He who has surpassed the greatness of
thought has passed beyond the contemplation of our eyes; for, he
says, "from Him and through Him and in Him are all things."[22] All

---

15 The concept of advancing from *feritas* to *humanitas* is frequent in classical
   Latin; cf. Lucretius 5.927; Cicero, *De officiis* 3.6.32.
16 Isa. 66.2.
17 Isa. 45.6-7.
18 Cf. the pantheistic view of Nature, held especially by the Stoics, in Cicero,
   De natura deorum 1.36.100. Zeno, the founder of Stoicism, stated that
   Nature was, with regard to the universe, "non artificiosa solum, sed plane
   artifex" (*ibid.* 2.22.58).
19 Rom. 1.20.
20 Cf. Tertullian, *De anima* 18.
21 1 Tim. 1.17.
22 Rom. 11.36.

things exist by His command, so that they are "from Him"; they are set in order by His word and are therefore "through Him." Finally, all things have recourse to His judgment so that, while they long for freedom "in Him," after corruption has been done away with, they appear to be recalled "to Him."

Chapter 4

The Lord rightly declares that God alone is good,[1] of whose goodness the whole world is a witness. He would not have created it if He were not good. For if "all things were very good,"[2] it logically follows that not only do those things which were created good prove the Creator is good, but they also prove that those things which owe their origin to a good creator cannot be other than good themselves. All evil, therefore, is a departure from God. (2) It is impossible that He who claims for Himself the title of perfect Father and Judge would be the instigator or author of any form of evil, precisely because He is the Judge and the Avenger of every evil deed. Man encounters evil only by his departure from the good God. (3) This very departure is blameworthy in man, not because it was necessary but because man himself willed it. Hence it was made clear to us not only what evil was but also from whom evil had taken its origin, lest there should seem to be envy in God.

(4) He is always, therefore, equal to Himself; He never changes[3] or transforms Himself into other forms, lest through change He should appear to be also mortal. For the modification implied in change from one thing to another involves a share in death of some sort. Therefore there is never any addition of parts or of glory in Him, lest anything should seem to have ever been wanting to the perfect one. Nor can there be any question of diminution in Him, for that would imply that some degree of mortality is in Him. On the contrary, what He is, He always is; who He is He always is; such as He is, He always is. (5) For increase in growth indicates a beginning; whereas any wasting away evidences death and destruction.

1 Cf. Luke 18.19
2 Gen. 1.31.
3 James 1.17.

And therefore He says: "I am God, and have not changed."[4] He always retains His manner of Being, because what is not born is not subject to change. (6) For—whatever that Being may be that is God[5]—this must always be true of Him, that He always is God, preserving Himself by His own powers. And therefore He says: "I am who am."[6] That which is has this name because it always preserves its same manner of being. Change takes away the name, "That which is"; for whatever changes at all is shown to be mortal by the very fact that it changes. It ceases to be what it was and consequently begins to be what it was not. (7) Of necessity, then, God always retains His manner of being, because He is always like unto Himself, always equal to Himself without any loss arising from change. For that which is not born cannot change, since only those things undergo change which are made or which are begotten; whereas things which at one time were not, experience existence by coming into being, and by coming into being they undergo change. On the contrary, things which have neither birth nor maker are exempt from change because they have not a beginning, the cause of change.

(8) And so God is said to be also unique since He has no equal. For God (whatever that Being may be that is God) must necessarily be supreme. Now whatever is supreme must be supreme in such wise that an equal is excluded. Therefore He must be the one and only Being with whom nothing can be compared, because He has no equal. (9) As the very nature of things demands, there cannot be two infinities. That alone is infinite which has absolutely neither beginning nor end; for whatever occupies the whole excludes the beginning of another. If the infinite does not contain all that exists (whatever it be), then it will find itself within that which contains it and therefore it will be less than the containing element. Hence it will cease to be God, since it has been brought under the dominion of

---

4 Mal. 3.6.
5 Novatian uses the expression *quod est deus* (frequent in Hilary) for the abstract *deitas,* which word is not found prior to Arnobius and Augustine.
6 Exod. 3.14.

another whose magnitude will include it because it is the smaller. As a result what contained it would itself claim to be God.

(10) It results from this that God's own name is ineffable because it cannot even be conceived. The name of a thing connotes whatever comes under the demands of its nature. For a name is significant of the reality which could be grasped from the name. However, when it is a question of something of such a nature that not even the intellectual powers themselves can form a proper concept, then how will it be expressed fittingly by a single word of designation, for it so exceeds the intellect that it is necessarily beyond the comprehension of any name? (11) When God takes for Himself a name or manifests it for certain reasons and on certain occasions, we know that it is not so much the real nature of the name that has been made known to us as a vague symbol appointed for our use, to which men may have recourse and find that they can appeal to God's mercy through it.

(12) God is, therefore, immortal and incorruptible, experiencing neither diminution nor end of any sort. Because He is incorruptible, He is also immortal, and because He is immortal, He is therefore also incorruptible. Both attributes are reciprocally linked together between and in themselves by a mutual relationship. Thus are they brought by the ensuing union to the condition of eternity: immortality proceeding from incorruptibility and incorruptibility coming from immortality.

Chapter 5

If in Scripture we consider instances of His legitimate wrath and descriptions of His anger and learn of the instances recorded of His hatred, we are not to regard these things asserted of Him as examples of human vices.[1] (2) Although all these things can corrupt man, they cannot vitiate the divine power in any way. Passions such as these are rightly said to exist in man but would wrongly be declared to exist in God. Man can be corrupted by them be-

1 Cf. Gregory of Elvira, *Tractatus Origenis* 1, lines 290-332, esp. 318-22 (ed. Bulhart, CCL 69.11-12). Novatian's text is quoted at least nine times in these homilies, the work of the Spanish writer Gregory (d. after 392) even though passing under the name of Origen.

cause he is capable of corruption; God cannot be corrupted by them because He is not capable of corruption. (3) Therefore they have a power of their own which they can exercise only where they find passible matter, not where they find an impassible substance. (4) The fact also that God is angry does not arise from any vice in Him; rather He acts thus for our benefit. He is merciful even when He threatens, because by these threats men are recalled to the right path. Fear is necessary for those who lack an incentive to good living, so that they who have rejected reason may at least be moved by terror. And so all these instances of anger, hatred, and the like, on God's part, are revealed, as the truth of the matter shows, for our healing and arise from deliberate purpose, neither from vice (5) nor from weakness. Therefore they do not have the power to corrupt God. The different elements of which we are made are wont to arouse in us the discord of anger which corrupts us; but this diversity of elements cannot exist in God either by nature or from vice, because He cannot conceivably be made up of a union of corporeal parts. (6) He is simple, without any corporeal admixture—whatever be the total of the being that only He Himself knows—since He is called spirit.[2] Thus those things which are faulty and the cause of corruption in man, inasmuch as they arise from the corruptibility of his body and matter itself, cannot exercise their power of corruptibility in God. As we have already said, they did indeed spring not from any vice in Him but from reason.

Chapter 6

Although heavenly Scripture frequently changes the divine countenance to human form when it says: "The eyes of the Lord are upon the just";[1] or "The Lord God smelled the scent of a good fragrance"[2] or "tables written with the finger of God"[3] are given to

2 John 4.24.

---

1 Ps. 33(34).16.
2 Gen. 8.21.
3 Exod. 31.18.

Moses; or the children of Israel are delivered from the land of Egypt "with a mighty hand and uplifted arm."[4] Again Scripture asserts: "The mouth of the Lord has spoken these things";[5] or when the earth is considered "the footstool of God";[6] or when it says: "Incline your ear, and hear."[7] We who say "that the law is spiritual"[8] do not confine the measure or form of the Divine Majesty within these outlines of our own bodily frame. On the contrary, we extend it infinitely over the field, if I may use the expression, of its own illimitable greatness. (2) For it is written: "If I ascend into heaven, You are there; if I descend into hell, You are present; and if I take my wings and depart across the sea, there shall Your hand take hold of me, and Your right hand hold me fast."[9] We know the meaning of Holy Scripture from the unfolding of the Divine Dispensation. The prophet, at that time, was still speaking about God in parables according to the faith of the times,[10] not as God really was, but as the people were able to comprehend Him. The use of such language to describe God must be attributed to the people, not to God.[11] (3) Thus the people were permitted to erect the tabernacle, although God cannot be contained within a tabernacle. The temple was constructed, although God cannot possibly be enclosed within the narrow limits of a temple. God is not finite, but the people's faculty of perceiving is finite. God is not straitened, but rather the understanding of people's minds is straitened. (4) Accordingly, Our Lord said in the Gospel: "The hour shall come, when neither on this mountain nor in Jerusalem will you worship the Father," and He gave the reason: "God is spirit, and therefore they who worship Him must worship in spirit and in truth."[12] (5) Thus it is

4 Ps. 135(136).12; Deut. 5.15.
5 Isa. 1.20.
6 Isa. 66.1.
7 4 Kings (2 Kings) 19.16.
8 Rom. 7.14.
9 Ps. 138(139).8-10.
10 The language of the prophets was parabolic, adapted to the understanding of the people, which was finite.
11 The people, not God, must be held accountable for the application of such anthropomorphic language to God.
12 John 4.21, 24.

the divine powers that are represented there by means of bodily members, and neither any external appearance nor bodily features of God are set before us. When eyes are ascribed to God, it is implied that He sees all things;[13] an ear, to show that He hears all things;[14] a finger,[15] to reveal a certain signification of the will; nostrils, to show that He is aware of our prayers as one is of odors;[16] hands,[17] to prove that He is the Author of every created thing; an arm,[18] to make it known that no nature can resist His power; and finally feet,[19] to make it clear that He fills all things, and that there is no thing in which God is not. (6) He does not have members, nor are the functions of members necessary to Him at whose will alone, even though it be unexpressed, all things serve and are present.[20] Why should He, who is light, have need of eyes? Why should He, who is everywhere, seek to procure feet? Why would He want to walk, when He can go nowhere outside Himself? Why should He desire hands, whose silent Will is the artificer of all things to be created? Nor does He, who knows even our secret wishes, have need of ears. Why should He need a tongue, whose very thought is a command? (7) These members were necessary to men, not to God, because man's purpose would have been ineffective if the body did not execute his thought. They are not necessary to God, whose works not only immediately follow His Will without any effort, but even proceed simultaneously with His Will. (8) Moreover, He is all eye because there is not a part of Him that does not see; all ear, because there is not a part of Him that does not hear; all hand, because there is not a part of Him that is not operative; all foot, because He is everywhere in His entirety. Likewise, the entirety of His being, whatever it may be, which contains no differentiation of parts, is everywhere in its entirety. (9) For whatever is simple does not admit of diversity within itself. Only those things

13 Cf. Ps. 33(34).16.
14 Cf. 4 Kings (2 Kings) 19.16.
15 Cf. Exod. 31.18.
16 Cf. Gen. 8.21.
17 Cf. Ps. 135(136).12; Deut. 5.15.
18 Cf. ibid.
19 Cf. Isa. 66.1.
20 Cf. Ps. 118(119).91.

which proceed from birth to dissolution are resolved into diversity
of members. Those things which are not composite cannot experience this; for what is immortal, whatever it is, must be one, simple,
and eternal. Since it is one, it cannot be dissolved because it lies
outside the law of dissolution, and it is not subject to the law of
death.

Chapter 7

When Our Lord affirms that God is spirit[1] I think that Christ
spoke thus about the Father because He wanted to imply that something more is to be understood than merely that God is spirit. Although He reasons with men in His Gospel in order to better their
understanding, nevertheless, even He speaks to men about God only
in a manner that they can perceive or grasp at the time. As we have
said, He endeavors to broaden their religious conceptions and bring
them to an acknowledgment of God. (2) We find it has been written
that "God" is called "love";[2] however, it does not follow from this
that the substance of God is expressed in the term love. Again,
because He is called "light,"[3] it does not follow that the substance
of God is contained in this expression. But all this is said of God
because that is all that can be expressed in words. Therefore, when
He is called spirit, one does not state all that He really is; He is so
called in order that man's mind may progress through a better understanding even to the concept of spirit. After the mind itself has
undergone a change in spirit, it may be able through the Spirit to
conclude that God is something more [than mere spirit][4] (3) What
He is[5] (insofar as His true essence is concerned) cannot be expressed
by human speech, nor perceived by human ears, nor grasped by
human senses. "If neither eye has seen nor ear heard, nor has the
heart of man nor his very mind perceived the things which God has

1 Cf. John 4.24.
2 1 John 4.8.
3 1 John 1.5.
4 Cf. 2 Cor. 3.15-18. Novatian is endeavoring to demonstrate the absolute
  immateriality of God.
5 Cf. Exod. 3.14.

prepared for them that love Him,"[6] what must He be, and how
great must He be who promises these things which the mind and the
nature of man fail to comprehend? (4) Furthermore, if you take
spirit to be the substance of God, you make God a created thing
because every spirit is a created thing. Therefore it would follow that
God was made. Likewise, if you claim according to Moses that God
is fire,[7] in saying that He is a creature, you have already described
something created; and you have not pointed out that He is its
Creator. (5) These expressions are used figuratively, rather than liter-
ally. For in the Old Testament, God is called fire to strike fear in the
hearts of a sinful people by appearing as their Judge; whereas in the
New Testament He is revealed as a spirit, that the Renewer and
Creator of those who are dead in their sins[8] may be acknowledged
by the goodness of His mercy granted to those who believe.

Chapter 8

Therefore this is the God whom the Church, rejecting as she does
the fables and the fancies of the heretics, acknowledges and vener-
ates. All nature, whether visible or invisible, gives unceasing witness
to Him. Angels adore Him, stars wonder at Him, seas bless Him,
lands revere Him, and even the lower regions look up at Him.[1] Every
human mind is conscious of Him, even though it cannot express Him.
All things move at His command: springs gush forth, rivers flow, waves
surge, all creatures bring forth their offspring. Winds are compelled to
blow, rains come, seas are stirred, all things pour forth their fruitfulness
everywhere. (2) He created for the special occupation of our first
parents a Paradise[2] in the East as a world of eternal life. He planted
the "tree of life" and in like manner set there another tree of the
"knowledge of good and evil."[3] He gave a command and pro-

6 1 Cor. 2.9.
7 Deut. 4.24.
8 Eph. 2.1.

---

1 Cf. Rom. 1.20; Ps. 96(97).1-7.
2 Gen. 2.8. For "first parents" Novatian uses the term *protoplasti* (literal-
   ly "first-formed"), already used by Tertullian, *De exhortatione castitatis*
   2.6 (CCL 2.1017).
3 Gen. 2.9.

nounced a sentence against any transgression.[4] He saved Noah,[5] who was a very just man, from the perils of the flood because of his innocence and faith. He took Enoch,[6] admitted Abraham to His friendship,[7] protected Isaac,[8] and made Jacob prosperous.[9] He placed Moses[10] at the head of His people, delivered the groaning children of Israel from the yoke of slavery,[11] wrote the Law, and led the descendants of the patriarchs into the land of promise.[12] (3) He instructed the prophets by His Spirit and through all of them promised His Son, Christ; and He sent Him at the time He had solemnly promised to give Him. He willed that through Christ we should come to a knowledge of Him; He also lavished upon us the abundant treasures of His mercy by giving His Spirit to enrich the poor and downtrodden. (4) And because He is so generous, benevolent, and good, lest this whole world should wither after it had turned away the streams of His grace, He willed that apostles as spiritual fathers of our human race be sent by His Son into the entire world,[13] so that poor humanity might acknowledge its Creator. If it should choose to follow Him, the human race would have One whom they could now address is their prayers as Father,[14] instead of God. (5) His providence has run and at present runs its course not only among individual men but also through whole cities and states, whose overthrow He predicted by the words of the prophets. In fact, His providence runs its course even through the whole world itself. He has described as consequences of its unbelief the world's punishment, its plagues, losses, and final fate. (6) And lest anyone should think that this indefatigable providence of God does not also embrace the least things, the Lord said: "One of two sparrows shall not fall to the

4 Cf. Gen. 2.16-17.
5 Cf. Gen. 6.8 ff.; 2 Peter 2.5.
6 Cf. Gen. 5.24.
7 Cf. Gen. 17.2-4.
8 Cf. Gen. 22.12.
9 Cf. Gen. 30.43.
10 Cf. Exod. 3.10.
11 Cf. Exod. 13.14; cf. 20.2.
12 Cf. Gen. 15.7; Jos. 1.2.
13 Matt. 28.19; Mark 16.15; Eph. 4.11.
14 Matt. 6.9; Luke 11.2.

ground without the Father's Will; for even the very hairs of your head are all numbered."[15] His care and providence neither allowed the garments of the Israelites to perish, nor the worthless shoes on their feet to wear out;[16] nor, finally, did He permit the wide trousers[17] of the captive young men to be burnt. And this is not without reason for if He who contains all things[18] embraces all things (all things, however, and the whole sum are made up of individual parts), then it follows logically that His care will be bestowed on every individual part because His providence extends to the whole, whatever it be.[19]

(7) That is the reason He also "sits above the Cherubim";[20] that is, He presides over His various works. The living creatures, which hold dominion over the rest, are subject to His throne; and the crystal from above[21] covers all things. In other words, all things are covered over by the heavens, made by God's command into a solid firmament[22] from the fluid material of the waters, that the thick ice, hardened by the frost, might form a division between the waters which formerly covered the earth and bear upon its back, so to speak, the weight of the water above the earth. (8) The wheels that lie beneath it[23] signify the various periods of time in which all the component members of the world are constantly being whirled forward. Furthermore, feet have been given to these members that they may not always stand still, but move on. (9) All their limbs are studded with eyes[24] because the works of

15 Matt. 10.29-30; Luke 12.6-7.
16 Cf. Deut. 8.4; 29.4.
17 Cf. Dan. 3.94.
18 Cf. Wisd. 1.7.
19 Although God is transcendent, He is not a stranger to this world, as the Marcionites claimed.
20 Ps. 79(80).2; 98(99).1; Dan. 3.55.
21 Cf. Rev. 4.6.
22 Cf. Gen. 1.6.
23 Cf. Ezech. 1.15 ff.; 10.9.
24 Cf. Ezech. 1.18; 10.12; Rev. 4.6.

God are to be contemplated with ever careful observation. And within their very bosom is a fire of glowing coals,[25] to signify that this world is hastening to the fiery day[26] of judgment, or that all the works of God are fiery, and not obscure,[27] but full of vigor; or for fear that these beings that have sprung from terrestrial beginnings would naturally grow numb because of the rigid nature of their origin. All were endowed, therefore, with the warm nature of an interior spirit, so that this warm nature mingling with their frigid bodies might supply all of them with proportionate constitutions for the exercise of life.[28] (10) This according to David, is God's chariot. "The chariot of God," he says, "is multiplied ten times a thousand times";[29] that is, it is incalculable, infinite, immeasurable. Under the yoke of the natural law which was given to all, some things are checked, as though they were drawn back by reins; whereas others are driven forward, as though they were urged on by slackened reins. (11) The world, this chariot of God and all that is therein, is guided by the angels[30] and the stars. Although their movements are varied—bound, nevertheless, by fixed laws—we see them guided to their goals according to the time measured out to them. So may we deservedly cry out with the Apostle as we admire the Maker and His works: "Oh, the depth of the riches of the wisdom and the knowledge of God; how inscrutable are His judgments and how unsearchable His ways,"[31] and the rest of the passage.

25 Cf. Ezech. 1.13.
26 2 Peter 3.12. For a study of the Stoic and patristic evolution of the world and final conflagration, see Spanneut, *op. cit.* 357-62.
27 Cf. John 3.19-21.
28 Novatian offers here a unique cosmic theory of Stoic inspiration (Spanneut, *op. cit.* 340-41).
29 Ps. 67(68).18.
30 Cf. Ps. 103(104).4. For the cosmic role of the angels in the Fathers, see Spanneut, *op. cit.* 329-30; J. Daniélou, *The Angels and Their Mission According to the Fathers of the Church* (Westminster, Md., 1957) 3-4.
31 Rom. 11.33.

Chapter 9

The same Rule of Truth teaches us, after we believe in the Father,
to believe also in the Son of God, Christ Jesus, the Lord Our God,[1]
nevertheless the Son of God. We are to believe in the Son of this
God who is the one[2] and only God; namely, the Creator of all
things, as has already been set forth above. (2) For we read that this
Jesus Christ, the Son, I repeat, of this God, was not only promised in
the Old Testament, but also has been manifested in the New Testament, fulfilling the shadows and types of all the prophecies[3] concerning the presence of His Incarnate[4] Truth. (3) The ancient prophecies and the Gospels alike bear witness that He is the Son of Abraham, that He is the Son of David.[5] (4) Even Genesis bears witness to
Him when it asserts: "To you will I give it and to your seed";[6] it
bears witness to Him when it describes how a man wrestled with
Jacob[7] and finally, when it states: "A prince shall not fail from
Judah, nor a ruler from his thighs, until He shall come to whom it
has been promised, and He shall be the expectation of nations."[8]
(5) Moses bears witness to Him, when he says: "Look for another to
send"[9] and again, when he testifies: "God shall raise up a prophet for
you from your brethren: give heed to him, as it were to me."[10] He

1 Novatian refers frequently to the baptismal Symbol of the Roman Church;
   all the elements of this baptismal Creed in Novatian have been gathered for
   us by L. P. Caspari, *Ungedruckte, unbeachtete und wenig beachtete
   Quellen zur Geschichte des Taufsymbols und der Glaubensregel* (Christiania
   1875) 3.463-65; for an abridged form, see A. D'Alès, *Novatien: Etude sur
   la théologie romaine au milieu du IIIe siècle* (Paris 1925) 135-37.
2 Fausset, in his edition (p. 28 n.26), feels that the word *unus* formed part of
   Novatian's Creed; it was preserved here and omitted above in 1.1; in 16.5
   Novatian writes "unum verum Deum."
3 See J. De Ghellinck *et al., Pour l'histoire du mot "Sacramentum"* (Louvain
   1924) 219.
4 "Corporatae veritatis." Cf. the *Verbum Corporatum* of the Sixteenth
   Council of Toledo (693 A. D.).
5 Cf. Matt. 1.1; Luke 3.23-38.
6 Gen. 17.8.
7 Cf. Gen 32.25.
8 Gen. 49.10.
9 Exod. 4.13.
10 Deut. 18.15.

bears witness of Him, finally, when he says: "You shall see your life hanging by night and day and shall not believe Him."[11] (6) Isaiah says of Him: "A rod shall go forth from the root of Jesse, and a flower shall rise up out of his root."[12] He refers to the same, when he says: "Behold a virgin shall conceive and bear a Son."[13] Isaiah bears witness to Him when he sets before us the works of healing that were to be done by Him: "Then shall the eyes of the blind be opened, and the ears of the deaf shall hear; then shall the lame man leap as the hart, and tongue of the dumb shall be eloquent."[14] He testifies of Him when he manifests His miracles of forbearance: "His voice shall not be heard in the public squares; a bruised reed He shall not break, and smoking flax He shall not quench."[15] (7) He refers to Him again when he describes His Gospels:[16] "I will make with you an everlasting covenant, the holy and sure promises of David."[17] He bears witness to Him when He prophesies that the Gentiles shall believe in Him: "Behold, I have made Him a leader and a master to the Gentiles. The nations which have not known You shall call upon You, and the peoples that know You not shall flee to You."[18] He bears witness to Christ, when referring to His Passion, he cries out: "He was led as a sheep to the slaughter, and as a lamb before His shearer is dumb; so He opened not His mouth in His lowliness."[19] (8) He bore witness to Him when he described the blows and stripes of His scourging: "By His bruises we were healed";[20] likewise, when he described His utter humiliation: "And we beheld Him, and He had no beauty or comeliness. A man in

11 Deut. 28.66. The Fathers of the Church often give this passage a Messianic interpretation; cf. Irenaeus, *Adv. haer.* 5.18.3; Tertullian(?), *Adv. Iudaeos* 11; Cyprian, *Testimonia* 2.20; and Pelikan, *Christian Tradition* . . . 1.62.
12 Isa. 11.1.
13 Isa. 7.14.
14 Isa. 35.5-6.
15 Isa. 42.2-3.
16 Isaiah is often called the Evangelist of the redemption.
17 Isa. 55.3.
18 Isa. 55.4-5.
19 Isa. 53.7-8.
20 Isa. 53.5.

affliction and who knows how to bear infirmity."[21] He bore witness
that the people would not believe in Him: "I have stretched forth
My hands all the day long to an unbelieving people."[22] He foretells
that He would rise again from the dead: "And in that day there shall
be a root of Jesse and one who shall rise to rule the Gentiles: in
Him shall the Gentiles hope, and His resting place shall be worthy
of honor."[23] The time of His Resurrection is indicated: "We
shall find Him ready, as it were, at daybreak."[24] He shall sit
at the right hand of the Father: "The Lord says to My Lord, 'Sit
at My right hand till I make Your enemies Your footstool' ",[25] and
He is represented as the possessor of all things: "Ask of Me and I will
give You the nations for your inheritance and the ends of the earth
for Your possession."[26] Finally, He is shown to be the Judge of all:
"O God, give the King Your judgment, and Your justice to the king's
son."[27] (9) I shall not pursue the matter further at this point; for
the things proclaimed about Christ are known to all heretics, and are
more than familiar to those who hold the truth.

Chapter 10

I must warn you that no other Christ should have been sought for
in the Gospel than this one who was promised before by the Creator
in the writings of the Old Testament, especially because the things
that were predicted about Him have been fulfilled, and all that has
been fulfilled was predicted beforehand. (2) To that counterfeit and
spurious Christ, devised somehow from old wives' tales by heretics[1]
who reject the authority of the Old Testament, I can, with reason,
truly and boldly say: Who are you? From what place did you
come? By whom were you sent? Why did you wish to come now? [2]

21 Isa. 53.2-3.
22 Isa. 65.2.
23 Isa. 11.10.
24 Hosea 6.3.
25 Ps. 109(110).1.
26 Ps. 2.8.
27 Ps. 71(72).1.

1 Namely, the Docetae (especially Marcion and his follower Apelles) and the
  Gnostics.
2 A reference to the suddenness of the descent of the heavenly Christ
  according to Marcion; cf. Tertullian, *Adv. Marc.* 4.11.

Why are you what you are? By what way did you manage to come? (3) Why did you not go to your own people, if not to prove, by coming among strangers that you have no people of your own? What have you to do with the Creator's world, or with man, the Creator's handiwork, or with the semblance of a body to which you deny the hope of resurrection? Why do you come to another man's servant,[3] and why do you desire to disturb another man's son? Why are you trying to take me away from the Lord? [4] Why do you drive me to blaspheme against the Father and make me impious? (4) Or what will I obtain from you in the resurrection, if, when I lose my body, I do not get myself back? If you wish to save, you should have made man to whom you could give salvation. If you desire to deliver me from sin, you should have granted me the grace beforehand not to fall into sin. What approval of the Law do you carry about with you? What testimony for your stand have you in the voice of the prophets? (5) Or what genuine good can I promise myself from you, when I see that you have come as a phantom and not in reality? And if you hate the body, what are you doing with the semblance of a body? In fact, you are proved false[5] in your claim to hate carrying about with you the substance of a body when you did not hesitate to assume the very semblance of one. For you ought to have hated even the imitation of a body, if you hated its reality. If you are another, you should have come in a different manner, so that you would not be called the Creator's son by your possession of even the appearance of flesh and body. Surely, if birth was odious to you because you hated the Creator's ordinance of marriage, you should have refused to assume even the very resemblance of a man born according to the Creator's ordinance of marriage.[6]

(6) Nor, in fact, do we acknowledge the Christ of the heretics, who existed (as they say) in appearance and not in reality. If he were a phantom and not reality, then he did not really perform any of these

---

3 Cf. Rom. 14.4.
4 Cf. *Adv. Marc.* 1.23.
5 The argument hinges on the fact that Christ Himself is *ipsa Veritas*; cf. Augustine, *De continentia* 10.24.
6 This heretical condemnation of marriage was based on the Gnostic conception of the essential evilness of matter.

actions that he is said to have performed. Nor do we acknowledge him to be Christ who in no way took upon himself our human body, inasmuch as he took nothing from Mary and consequently never came to us because he was not seen in our own bodily substance when he appeared. Finally, we do not acknowledge him to be a Christ who put on ethereal or sidereal flesh, as other heretics[7] would have it, lest we should see any salvation[8] of ours in him, if we did not also recognize the real substance of our own body. And we utterly reject anyone else who bears a body of any other kind whatever of heretical figment. (7) Not only Our Lord's Nativity but even His death refutes all these heretics. "And the Word," says John, "was made flesh and dwelt among us";[9] consequently, He must have had our human body because the Word truly took our flesh. Blood flowed from His hands and feet and even from His very side, that He might prove Himself to be a sharer of our human body by dying according to the laws of our human dissolution. (8) The wounds of His very body proved that He was raised again from the dead in the same corporeal substance in which He died. Thus He showed us the conditions of our resurrection in His own flesh, by restoring in His Resurrection the same body which He had from us. Hence a law of resurrection is laid down because Christ is raised up in the substance of His body as a model for others. (9) Because it is written: "Flesh and blood shall not obtain the kingdom of God,"[10] it is not meant that the substance of our flesh, which was fashioned by the hands of God so as not to perish, was condemned. On the contrary, only the guilt of the flesh is censured, the guilt which was caused by man's deliberate and rash rebellion against the claims of divine law. After this guilt has been taken away in baptism and in the dissolution brought about by death, then the flesh is restored to salvation, because the flesh is recalled to a state of innocence,[11] after the mortal condition of sin has been put aside.

---

7 The Syrian Gnostics Saturninus or Satornil, and others. According to Tertullian (*De carne Christi* 6.8), Apelles attributed a sidereal body to Christ.

8 The Docetae compromised the reality of Christ's passion and thereby the value of the redemption.

9 John 1.14.

10 1 Cor. 15.50.

11 Cf. Tertullian, *De baptismo* 5.

Chapter 11

Lest we seem—by our assertion that Our Lord Jesus Christ, the Son of God the Creator, manifested Himself in the substance of a real body—to have joined forces with or given material for controversy to other heretics,[1] who in this connection maintain that He was solely and simply a man and who therefore are very eager to prove that He was a mere man and nothing more, we do not express ourselves in such a manner concerning the substance of His body and claim that He was simply and solely a man. On the contrary we maintain that, by the fact that the divinity of the Word was permixed in that very matter,[2] He was also God according to the Scriptures. (2) It is very dangerous to say of Christ—the Saviour of the human race, the Lord and Prince of the whole world, to whom "all things have been" entrusted and "granted by His Father,"[3] by whom all things were made, all things created, all things set in order, the King of all ages[4] and of all times, the Ruler of all the angels, before whom there was nothing besides the Father—to say that He is only man and to deny His divine authority in these things. This insult from the heretics will also extend to God the Father, if God the Father could not beget God the Son. (3) No blindness on the part of the heretics shall lay down the law for the truth. Because they maintain one thing about Christ and do not maintain the other, and because they see one side of Him and not the other, never shall the heretics take away from us the truth which they do not see for the sake of what they do see. (4) For they consider in Him the frailties of man, but they do not regard the powers of a God. They reflect on the infirmities of His flesh, but they exclude from their minds the powers of His divinity. If this proof drawn from the infirmities of Christ has such efficacy as to prove that He is man precisely because of those infirmities, then the proof of His divinity, drawn from His miracles, will have enough efficacy to show on account of His mighty works that He is also God. If His sufferings

---

1 The Adoptianists.
2 Cf. Cicero, *Tusculan Disputations* 1.27.66; Tertullian, *De anima* 52.
3 Matt. 11.27.
4 1 Tim. 1.17.

manifest human frailty in Him, why should not His works confirm
the divine power in Him? If the miracles do not suffice to prove
Him God, then neither will the sufferings alone suffice to prove Him
man. (5) Whatever principle is posited in either case will be found to
be suspect in the other. If it cannot be proved that He is God
because of His miracles, there will also be the danger of not being
able to show that He is man because of His sufferings. One must not
lean to one side and incline away from the other, for whoever rejects
a portion of the truth will never hold the complete truth. (6) Just as
Scripture proclaims that Christ is also God, so, too, does it proclaim
that God is very Man. It describes Jesus Christ as Man, just as it
describes Christ the Lord as God. Scripture proclaims Him to be not
only the Son of God but also the Son of Man; it not only calls Him
the Son of Man but has also been accustomed to refer to Him as the
Son of God, so that He is both because He is of both. Otherwise—if He
were only the one—He could not be the other. (7) Nature itself
demands that we believe that he is a man who is of man. Likewise it
demands that we believe that he is God who is of God;[5] otherwise, if
He were not also God, when He is of God, then He would not be
man, though He is of man. Both natures alike would be endangered
by the denial of one or the other, inasmuch as one proves to have
been discredited by the overthrow of the other. (8) Therefore, let
those who read in Scripture that the Man Christ Jesus is the Son of
Man, also read there that this same Jesus is called both God and Son
of God.[6] In the same manner that He, as Man, is of Abraham,[7] even
so, as God, is He also before Abraham[8] himself. In the same manner
that He, as Man, is the Son of David,[9] so is He also, as God, called
the Lord of David.[10] And in the same manner that He, as Man, is
made under the Law,[11] so is He also, as God, declared to be the

5 Cf. John 8.42.
6 Cf. 1 Tim. 2.5.
7 Cf. Matt. 1.1.
8 Cf. John 8.58.
9 Cf. Matt. 20.31; 22.42.
10 Cf. Matt. 22.43-45.
11 Cf. Gal. 4.4.

Lord of the Sabbath.[12] In the same manner that He, as Man, en-
dured the sentence of death, we find that, as God, He has all judgment over the living and the dead.[13] In the same manner that He, as
Man, is born after the world existed, so, as God, is He shown to have
existed before the world.[14] In the same manner that He, as Man, was
born "of the seed of David,"[15] so in like manner is it said that
through Him, as God, the world was made.[16] In the same manner
that He, as Man, was after many, He was, as God, before all men. In
the same manner that He, as Man, was lower in rank than the
others,[17] as God He was greater than all. In the same manner, that
He, as Man, ascended into heaven,[18] as God, He first descended from
heaven.[19] In the same manner that he, as Man, goes to the Father,[20]
so as a Son obedient to His Father shall he descend from the Father.
(9) Therefore, if limitations give evidence of human frailty in Him,
His majesty affirms His divine power. However, when you read
about both these truths, there is danger that you will believe not
both of them but only one. Since we read of both attributes in
Christ, we should believe both of them so that our faith may be true
only if it is also complete. (10) If one of these two truths ceases to
have a part in our faith, while the other truth (and precisely that
truth which is of lesser importance) is accepted as a matter of faith,
then the Rule of Truth has been shaken. Such temerity will not give
salvation; in its stead it will, through the rejection of faith, bring
about a serious danger of death.

Chapter 12

Why, then, should we hesitate to say what Scripture does not
hesitate to express? Why should the truth of Faith waver where the

12 Matt. 12.8; Mark 2.28; Luke 6.5.
13 Cf. John 5.22.
14 Cf. John 17.5.
15 Rom. 1.3.
16 John 1.10.
17 Cf. Isa. 53.3.
18 Cf. Mark 16.19; Luke 24.51; Acts 1.9.
19 Cf. John 6.38, 63.
20 Cf. John 14.3, 28; Acts 1.11.

authority of Scripture has never faltered? For behold, the prophet Hosea says in the person of the Father: "I will not save them by bow, nor by horses; but I will save them by the Lord their God."[1] (2) If God says that He will save them by God and if God does not save except by Christ, then why should man hesitate to call Christ God when he realizes that the Father declares, through the Scriptures, that He is God. In fact, if God the Father can not save, except by God, no one can be saved by God the Father, unless he has acknowledged that Christ is God, in whom and through whom the Father promises to grant salvation.[2] Consequently, whoever acknowledges that He is God, finds salvation in Christ who is God; whoever does not acknowledge that He is God, has lost salvation, which he cannot find elsewhere but in Christ who is God.

(3) For just as Isaiah says: "Behold a virgin shall conceive and bear a son, and you shall call His name Emmanuel,"[3] "which is interpreted 'God with us,' "[4] so too, does Christ Himself say: "Behold I am with you, even to the consummation of the world."[5] God, then, is with us, and what is more, He is even in us. Christ is with us; therefore it is He whose name is "God with us," because He is also with us. Or is it possible that He is not with us? Then, how can He say that He is with us? He is, therefore, with us, and because He is with us, He is called Emmanuel, "God with us." God, then, because He is with us, was called "God with us." (4) The same prophet says: "Be strong, you feeble hands and weak knees; be comforted, you that are faint-hearted, be strong, fear not. Behold, our God will render judgment: He will come and save us; then shall the eyes of the blind be opened, and the ears of the deaf shall hear; then shall the lame man leap as the hart, and the tongue of the dumb shall be eloquent."[6] (5) If the prophet says that these signs—which have

1 Hosea 1.7.
2 Cf. Acts 4.12.
3 Isa. 7.14. St. Justin (*Dialogus cum Tryphone* 67, 71, 84; tr. by T. B. Falls, FC 6.254, 263, 281f.). was the first Christian writer to defend, at length, the virginal conception of Mary contained in Isa. 7.14 against the Jewish interpretations.
4 Matt. 1.23.
5 Matt. 28.20.
6 Isa. 35.3-6.

already been wrought—will be the future signs of God's advent, then let the heretics either acknowledge that Christ is the Son of God, at whose coming and by whom these miracles of healing were wrought, or—defeated by the truth of Christ's divinity and falling into the other heresy,[7] inasmuch as they refuse to confess that Christ is the Son of God and God—let them confess that He is the Father. Since they have been restrained by the words of the prophets, they can no longer deny that Christ is God. (6) What, then, can they reply, when the miracles which were prophesied as taking place at the coming of God, were actually wrought at the advent of Christ? In what way do they think Christ is God? For they can no longer deny that He is God. Do they think He is the Father or the Son? If they accept Him as the Son, why do they deny that the Son of God is God? If they accept Him as the Father, why are they not following those who are seen to hold such blasphemies? At any rate, in this debate with them about the truth, it suffices for our present purpose that, no matter how they are refuted, they confess that Christ, whose divinity they wished to deny, is also God.

(7) He says through Habakkuk the prophet: "God shall come from the south, and the holy one from the dark and dense mountain."[8] Whom would they have come from the South? [9] If they say that God the Father almighty came, then God the Father came from a place; consequently, He is also enclosed by space and contained within the limits of some abode. Thus the sacrilegious heresy of Sabellius, as we said, takes concrete form because of these men who believe that Christ is not the Son but the Father. It is strange how these heretics, while insisting that Christ is a mere man, make an about-face and acknowledge that Christ is the Father, God almighty. (8) If Christ, who is also called God by the Scriptures, was born in Bethlehem, which geographically faces towards the South, then this God is rightly described as coming from the South, because it was foreseen that He would come from Bethlehem. (9) Therefore let

7 The Sabellian heresy.
8 Hab. 3.3.
9 According to Novatian, Christ is the God who comes *ab Africo*: "from the South (Bethlehem)" by synecdoche. Cf. Irenaeus, *Adv. haer.* 4.33.11.

them decide just who this Person from the South is, the Father or the Son? For Scripture says that God will come from the South. If He is the Son, why do they hesitate to say that Christ is also God, for Scripture says that God will come? If He is the Father, why do they hesitate to associate themselves with the rashness of Sabellius, who says that Christ is the Father? The truth of the matter is that, whether they call Him the Father or the Son, they are compelled, though against their will, to abandon their own heresy since they are accustomed to say that Christ is only a man. The very facts constrain them to declare that He is God, whether they choose to call Him the Father or the Son.

Chapter 13

In like manner, John, in his description of Christ's Nativity, says: "The Word was made flesh and dwelt among us. And we saw His glory—the glory as of the only-begotten of the Father—full of grace and of truth."[1] For "His name is called the Word of God"[2] also, and not without reason. "My heart," he says, "has uttered a good word," the word which he subsequently calls by the name of king, when he says: "I speak my works to the king."[3] (2) For "through Him all things were made, and without Him nothing was made."[4] "For whether they be Thrones," says the Apostle, "or Dominations, or Virtues, or Powers, all things, visible and invisible, exist through Him."[5] This is the Word who "came into His own and His own received Him not."[6] For "the world was made through Him, and the world knew Him not."[7] However, this "Word was in the beginning with God, and the Word was God."[8] (3) When John states in the latter part of his prologue that "the Word was made flesh and dwelt

1 John 1.14.
2 Rev. 19.13.
3 Ps. 44(45).2, quoted by Tertullian, *Adv. Praxean* 7, 11.
4 John 1.3.
5 Col. 1.16.
6 John 1.11.
7 John 1.10.
8 John 1.1.

among us,"[9] who can doubt that Christ, whose birth it is, and because He was made flesh, is Man? And because He is the Word of God, who can hesitate for a moment to declare that He is God, especially when one realizes that the Gospel account has associated both these natures in the unique union of Christ's Nativity? [10]

(4) He it is who "comes forth as a bridegroom from His bridal chamber and rejoiced as a giant to run His course; His going forth is from the highest heaven and His return even to the height thereof."[11] For He [returns] even to the height; "since no one has ascended into heaven except Him who has descended from heaven, the Son of Man who is in heaven."[12] He repeats this very same fact when He says: "Father, glorify Me with the glory that I had with You before the world existed."[13] (5) If this Word descended from heaven as a bridegroom to take on our flesh, so that in taking flesh He might ascend again as Son of Man to that place whence, as Son of God, the Word had descended, then assuredly, because of a mutual bond, the flesh bears the Word of God, and the Son of God assumes the weakness of the flesh. He ascends with His spouse, the flesh, to the same place from which He had descended without the flesh and receives now that glory which He is shown to have had before the creation of the world. This proves, without the least doubt, that He is God. Nevertheless, since the world itself is said to have been created after Him, it is evident that it was created through Him. This fact itself gives proof of the glory and the authority of the divinity that is in Him, through whom the world was made.

(6) Now if Christ sees the secrets of the heart,[14] Christ is certainly God, since God alone knows the secrets of the heart.[15] If the same

9 John 1.14.
10 Cf. Tertullian, *Adv. Prax.* 27.
11 Ps. 18(19).6-7. The mystical interpretation—Christ the "Groom" issued from Mary's womb—of this psalm in terms of the Incarnation is very ancient; cf. Irenaeus, *Adv. haer.* 4.33.13; Justin, *Apol.* 1.54 (tr. by Falls, FC 6.93); *Dial.* 64, 69, Tertullian, *Adv. Marc.* 4.11; Cyprian, *Test.* 2.19.
12 John 3.13.
13 John 17.5.
14 Cf. Matt. 9.4; John 2.25.
15 Cf. 3 Kings (1 Kings) 8.39.

Christ forgives sins, Christ is certainly God because no one can forgive sins but God alone.[16] If Christ came down from heaven in
coming into the world, Christ is certainly God, because no mere man
can come from heaven.[17] If the statement: "I and the Father are
one,"[18] can be said by no man and if Christ in the consciousness of
His divinity makes this statement, Christ is certainly God. If the
apostle Thomas, finally convinced by all the proofs and the facts of
Christ's divinity, says in reply to Christ: "My lord and My God,"[19]
Christ is certainly God. If the apostle Paul also writes in his epistles:
"Of whom are the fathers, and of whom is Christ according to the
flesh, who is over all things, God blessed forever,"[20] Christ is certainly God. If the same apostle declares that he is "an apostle sent not
from men by man, but by Jesus Christ,"[21] and asserts that "he
learned the Gospel not from men or through man, but received it
from Jesus Christ,"[22] Christ is certainly God.

(7) At this point, therefore, one of two alternatives must be true.
Since it is evident that all things were made through Christ, either He
is before all things, because "all things are through Him,"[23] and
consequently He is God, or else, because He is man, He is after all
things, and consequently nothing was made through Him. But we
cannot say that nothing was made through Him, since we know that
it is written: "All things were made through Him."[24] He is not after
all things; that is, He is not a mere man who is after all things; for He
is also God because God is before all things. He is before all things
because "all things are through Him";[25] otherwise, were He only a
man, nothing would be through Him. On the other hand, if all things
were made through Him, He would not be a mere man. Were He
merely a man, all things would not be made through Him; in fact,

16 Cf. Matt. 9.2; Mark 2.5; Luke 5.20.
17 Cf. John 3.13.
18 John 10.30.
19 John 20.28.
20 Rom. 9.5.
21 Gal. 1.1.
22 Cf. Gal. 1.11-12.
23 John 1.3.
24 *Ibid.*
25 *Ibid.*

nothing would be made through Him. (8) What, then, do the heretics reply: that nothing is through Him, hence He is a mere man? Then, how are all things through Him? Therefore He is not only Man but also God because all things are through Him. Consequently, we must understand not only that Christ is not a mere man who is after all things but that He is also God because all things were made through Him. Or how can you say that He is only man, when you behold Him also in the flesh? Certainly if both these truths are carefully considered, one must necessarily believe both truths.

Chapter 14

Yet the heretic still hesitates to say that Christ is God, even though he notes that it has been proved in so many words and by so many facts that He is God. (2) If Christ is only man, how did He "come unto His own"[1] when He came into this world, since man could not have made a world? (3) If Christ is only man, how is "the world" said to have been "made through Him,"[2] when it is stated, not that the world was created through man but that man was created after the world? (4) If Christ is only man, how is it that Christ is not only of the seed of David[3] but "the Word was made flesh, and dwelt among us"?[4] Though the first man was not born of human seed,[5] still he was not compounded from the union of the Word and flesh, simply because he is not "the Word made flesh, [who] dwelt among us."[6] (5) If Christ is only man, how does "He who comes down from heaven bear witness to that which He has seen and heard,"[7] when it is evident that man cannot come from heaven because he cannot be born there? (6) If Christ is only man, how are "things visible and invisible, Thrones, Virtues and Dominations" said to have been "created through Him and in Him,"[8] when the heavenly pow-

1 John 1.11.
2 John 1.10.
3 Rom. 1.3.
4 John 1.14.
5 Gen. 2.7; cf. John 1.13.
6 John 1.14.
7 John 3.31-32.
8 Col. 1.16.

ers could not have been created through man, since they must have existed before man? (7) If Christ is only man, how is He present wherever He is invoked[9] —since it is not man's nature but God's to be able to be present everywhere? (8) If Christ is only man, why is a man called upon in prayer as a mediator, when calling upon a man to grant salvation is considered useless? (9) If Christ is only man, why is hope put in Him,[10] when hope in man is declared to be accursed?[11] (10) If Christ is only man, why cannot He be denied without ruin to one's soul,[12] when it is declared that an offense against man can be forgiven? [13] (11) If Christ is only man, how does John the Baptist bear witness of Him when he says: "He who comes after me was made before me, for He was before me"? [14] If Christ were only man, then, being born after John, He could not be before John, unless he preceded him as God. (12) If Christ is only man, how is it that "what the Father does, the Son also does in like manner,"[15] when man cannot do works like the heavenly works of God? (13) If Christ is only man, how is it that "as the Father has life in Himself, so has He given to the Son to have life in Himself," [16] when man cannot have life in himself after the manner of God the Father, because he is not glorious in eternity, but is made with the perishable matter of mortality? (14) If Christ is only man, how could He say: "I am the bread of eternal life that came down from heaven,"[17] when man who is himself mortal neither can be the bread of life, nor has descended from heaven, since no matter of frailty can be found in heaven? (15) If Christ is only man, how does He assert: "For no man has ever seen God the Father; but He who is from God, He has seen"[18] God? For if Christ is only man, He could not have seen God because "no man has seen God."[19] If He has seen

9 Cf. Matt. 18.20.
10 Cf. 1 Cor. 15.19; 1 Tim. 1.1.
11 Cf. Jer. 17.5.
12 Cf. Matt. 10.33.
13 Cf. Matt. 6.14-15; 18.35; Mark 11.25; also 1 Kings (1 Sam.) 2.25.
14 John 1.15.
15 John 5.19.
16 John 5.26.
17 John 6.51.
18 Cf. John 6.46.
19 John 1.18; 1 John 4.12.

God because He is of God, then he wished Himself to be considered more than man since He has seen God. (16) If Christ is only man, why does He say: "What if you shall see the Son of Man ascending to that place where He was before?"[20] But He did ascend into heaven; therefore He was there before, in that He returned to the same place where He was before. (17) Now if He was sent from heaven by the Father, He certainly is not a mere man; for as we said, man could not come from heaven. Therefore He was not there before as man; He ascended to that place where as man He had not been. However the Word of God, who was there, descended—the Word, I say, of God who is also God, through whom "all things were made, and without whom nothing was made."[21] Thus it was not man that came thence from heaven but the Word of God, that is, God, descended from that place.

Chapter 15

If Christ is only man, how is it that He says: "Even if I bear witness to Myself, my witness is true, because I know where I came from and where I go. You judge according to the flesh"?[1] Note that He also says in this passage that He will return to the place from which He testified that He previously came—sent, namely, from heaven. Therefore He descended from the place from which He came, just as He goes to the place from which He descended. Consequently, if Christ were only man, He would not have come from that place and—since He had not come from that place—He could not return there. By coming, however, from that place from which man cannot come, He showed that He came as God. (2) But the Jews, ignorant and unacquainted, as they were, with this descent of His, made these heretics their heirs, addressing them with the very same words: You do not know from what place I come, nor where I go. You judge according to the flesh."[2] So these heretics, as well as the Jews, maintaining that the carnal birth of Christ was His only birth,

20 John 6.62.
21 John 1.3.

---

1 John 8.14-15.
2 *Ibid.*

believed that Christ was nothing else but a man. They do not reflect that since man could not come down from heaven, so as to be able accordingly to return to heaven, He who descended from heaven, whence man could not have come, is God.

(3) If Christ is only man, how does He say: "You are from below, I am from above; you are of this world; I am not of this world"? [3] Does it follow that Christ is a mere man simply because every man is of this world, and Christ, as one of them, is in this world? [4] Not at all! Rather, consider what He says: "I am not of this world."[5] Does He lie then? If He is only man, He is of this world. On the other hand, if He is not lying, He is not of this world. Therefore, He is not a mere man since He is not of this world. (4) In order that His identity might not remain unknown, He made it quite clear whence He was: "I", said He, "am from above";[6] that is, from heaven, whence man cannot come, for man was not made in heaven. He who is from above is God; therefore He is not of this world. In a certain sense, He is of this world; consequently, Christ is not only God, but also Man. Accordingly, just as He is not of this world according to the divinity of the Word, so is He of this world according to the frailty of the body which He assumed. Man is joined to God, and God is coupled to Man.[7] (5) However, in this passage Christ emphasized only one side, His divinity. Since the Jews in their blindness considered only the human side of Christ, in this passage He passed over in silence the fragility of the body, which is of this world, and spoke only of His divinity, which is not of this world. To the same extent that the Jews were inclined to believe that He was only man did Christ, on His part, draw them to consider His divinity so that they would believe He was God. He wished to overcome their incredulity regarding His divinity by omitting, for the time being, any mention of His human heritage and by simply placing before them His divinity alone.

3 John 8.23.
4 Cf. John 1.10.
5 John 8.23.
6 *Ibid.*
7 An early expression of what was later called the Hypóstatic Union.

(6) If Christ is only man, how does He say: "From God I came forth and have come,"[8] when it is a well-known fact that man was made by God and did not come forth from God? Man, then, did not come forth from God in the same manner that the Word of God came forth, concerning whom it is said: "My heart has brought forth a good Word."[9] Since this Word is from God, therefore, it is "with God";[10] and because it was not uttered without effect, it rightly does all things: "All things were made through Him and without Him, nothing was made."[11] Now this Word, through whom all things were made, [is God]. "And the Word," John says, "was God."[12] Therefore God proceeded from God, since the Word who proceeded is God who proceeded from God. (7) If Christ is only man, how does He say: "If any man keep my word, he will never see death"?[13] What is never seeing death but immortality? Immortality, however, is the companion of divinity because divinity is immortal, and immortality is the fruit of divinity.[14] Now every man is mortal; so immortality cannot come from what is mortal. Therefore immortality cannot derive its origin from Christ as mortal man. However, He says: "Whoever keeps my word will never see death."[15] Hence the word of Christ bestows immortality and through immortality bestows divinity.[16] If man, since he is himself mortal, cannot claim to make someone else immortal and if Christ's word not only claims but actually bestows immortality, then you can be certain that He who grants this immortality is not just a mere man. He could not bestow it, were He only a man. But He proves that He is God by bestowing divinity through immortality and by offering divinity which He could not bestow unless He were God.

(8) If Christ is only man, how does He say: "I am before Abraham"?[17] No man can be before him from whom he himself takes his

8 John 8.42.
9 Ps. 44(45).2.
10 John 1.1.
11 John 1.3.
12 John 1.1.
13 John 8.51.
14 Cf. Wisd. 6.19.
15 John 8.51. For the descent from Abraham, see Matt. 1.1-16.
16 Cf. 2 Peter 1.4.
17 John 8.58.

origin; nor is it possible that a thing existed before that from which
it itself took its origin. Yet, Christ, even though He descends from
Abraham, says that He is before Abraham. Either He is lying, therefore, and deceiving us (if He, who actually descended from Abraham,
was not before Abraham), or He is not deceiving us (if He is also God
because He was before Abraham). For if He had not been God, it is
evident that He could not have been before Abraham because He
had really descended from Abraham. (9) If Christ is only man, how
does He say: "And I shall know them, and my own follow Me; and I
give them everlasting life, and they shall never perish." [18] Now, every
man is bound by the laws of mortality and therefore cannot even
keep himself alive forever; much less can he keep another man alive
forever. Christ, nevertheless, promises to give salvation forever. And if
He does not give it, He is a liar; if He does give it, He is God. But He
does not deceive, for He gives what He promises. Therefore He is
God, who offers eternal salvation, which man, who cannot even save
himself, cannot grant to another.

(10) If Christ is only man, what does He mean when He says: "I
and the Father are one"? [19] How can "I and the Father be one," [20] if
He is not both God and Son, who therefore can be said to be one
thing [21] [with the Father] because He is of Him and because He is His
Son and because He is born of Him inasmuch as He is found to have
proceeded from Him? This proves that He is also God. (11) The Jews
considered this odious and believed that it was blasphemy, since
Christ had shown by these words that He was God. Therefore they
ran to get stones and passionately set about to cast them at Him. [22]
He vigorously refuted His adversaries with the precedent and testimony of the Scriptures. "If [the Law] called them gods," He says,
"to whom the words of God were addressed—and the Scripture cannot be broken—do you say to Me whom the Father has made holy
and sent into this world. 'You blaspheme,' because I said, 'I am the

18 John 10.27-28.
19 John 10.30.
20 *Ibid.*
21 *Unum.* Cf. Tertullian, *Adv. Prax.* 22.
22 Cf. John 10.31.

Son of God'? "[23] (12) With these words He did not deny that He was God; on the contrary he affirmed that He was God. If, beyond any question of a doubt, they are said to be gods to whom the words of God were addressed, much more is He God who is found to be better than all of them. And yet He refuted their slanderous blasphemy in a fitting manner by a proper ordering [of relations]; for He wants Himself to be considered God and considered precisely as the Son of God, not the Father Himself. In fact, He said that He was sent, and pointed out to them: "Many works have I shown you from My Father."[24] Therefore, He wanted Himself to be considered not the Father but the Son. Also, in the last part of His defense He made mention of the Son, not the Father: "You say, 'You blaspheme,' because I said, 'I am the Son of God.' "[25] (13) So, with regard to the charge of blasphemy, He answered that He was the Son, not the Father, whereas, in regard to His own divinity, He proved that He was the Son and God when He said: "I and the Father are one."[26] Therefore, He is God, but God in such a manner that He is the Son, not the Father.

Chapter 16

If Christ is only man, how is it that He himself says: "And whoever sees and believes in Me, shall never die"?[1] Whereas he who trusts in a mere man is said to be accursed,[2] he who believes in Christ is not accursed; on the contrary, it is stated that he will never die. Consequently, if He is only man, as the heretics would have it, how is it that whoever believes in Him shall never die, since he who trusts in man is considered accursed? Or if he is not accursed, but rather, as one reads, destined for the attainment of eternal life, Christ is not man only but God; and whoever believes in Him not only avoids the danger of such a curse but also attains to the fruit of justice.

23 John 10.35-36.
24 John 10.32.
25 John 10.36.
26 John 10.30.

1 John 11.26; 6.40.
2 Jer. 17.5.

(2) If Christ is only man, how does He say that the Paraclete will receive of what is His and will declare these things? [3] For the Paraclete does not receive anything from man, but rather gives knowledge to man. Nor does the Paraclete learn future things from man; He instructs him about things to come. Therefore, either the Paraclete did not receive from Christ, as Man, what He should make known, simply because man will never be able to give anything to the Paraclete, from whom he himself must receive (and in that case, Christ not only errs but also deceives in the present passage when He says that the Paraclete will receive from Him, as Man, the things which He will make known), or He does not deceive us— just as He does not deceive—and the Paraclete receives from Christ the things which He will make known. (3) If He received from Christ the things which He will make known, then surely Christ is greater than the Paraclete, since the Paraclete would not receive from Christ unless He were less than Christ. Now, the fact that the Paraclete is less than Christ proves that Christ is also God, from whom He received what He makes known. This, then, is a great testimony to Christ's divinity, inasmuch as the Paraclete, having been found to be less than Christ, takes from Him what He gives to others. If Christ were only man, Christ would receive from the Paraclete what He should say; the Paraclete would not receive from Christ what He should make known.

(4) If Christ is only man, why did He lay down for us a rule to be believed when He said: "Now this is everlasting life, that they may know Thee, the one and true God, and Jesus Christ, whom Thou hast sent"? [4] If He did not wish Himself to be considered also God, why did He add: "and Jesus Christ, whom Thou hast sent,"[5] unless He wished to be acknowledged also as God. If He did not wish Himself to be considered God, He would have added: "and the man Jesus Christ, whom Thou hast sent." As a matter of fact, He did not add anything; nor did Christ teach us in this present passage that He

3 John 16.14.
4 John 17.3.
5 *Ibid.*

was only man; He associated Himself with God. He wanted us to understand that He was, on account of this association, also God—as He truly is. (5) Therefore we must believe, according to the prescribed Rule, in the Lord, the one true God. Similarly we must believe in Him whom He has sent, Jesus Christ, who would never have associated Himself with the Father, as we have said, unless He had wished to be acknowledged also as God. He would have separated Himself from Him if He had not wished to be understood to be God. He would have ranked Himself only with men, if He had known that He was only man; and He would not have associated Himself with God, if He had not known that He was also God. Now He does not even mention His humanity, because no one doubts that He is man. He associates Himself with God, and rightly so, in order to lay down a formal statement of His divinity for those who were to believe in Him.

(6) If Christ is only man, how does He say: "And now glorify Me with the glory which I had with Thee before the world was"? [6] If He had glory with God before the world was and retained His glory with the Father, certainly He existed before the world. For He could not have had this glory unless He had existed before the world, so as to keep the glory. No one who possesses anything can have anything unless He exists before it. But Christ has glory before the creation of the world; therefore, He existed before the creation of the world. Unless He had existed before the creation of the world, He could not have had glory before the creation of the world, because He Himself would not have existed. In fact, man, who existed after the world, could not have glory before the creation of the world. Christ had it; therefore, He existed before the world. Consequently, He who existed before the world was not man only but God, for He existed before the world and possessed glory before the world existed.

(7) Nor can anyone say that it is a question here of predestination, since Scripture contains nothing to that effect. Let those who think this add it [to the written word]. However, woe is as much pro-

---

6 John 17.5. Novatian is contending with the Artemonites, who maintained that Jesus Christ was God only by predestination.

nounced upon those who add to, as upon those who take away from, what is written.[7] Therefore what cannot be added to the written word cannot be asserted. Accordingly, after we have eliminated the possibility of predestination because it is not contained in the written word, we conclude that Christ existed in substance before the creation of the world. In fact, He is "the Word" through whom "all things were made, and without whom nothing was made."[8] (8) Even if someone does say that He was glorious in predestination and that this predestination took place before the creation of the world, due order must be observed. And there will be a considerable number of men before Christ destined to glory. In such a determination to glory, Christ will be considered less than other men, because He is ranked after them in time. In fact, if this glory was in predestination, then Christ was the last to receive this predestination to glory; for we see that Adam was predestined before Him, as were also Abel, Enoch, Noah, Abraham, and the rest. (9) Since the order of all persons and things is at the disposal of God's arrangement, many will be said to have been predestined to glory before the predestination of Christ. Accordingly, Christ is found to be less than other men, He who is really better and greater and more ancient even than the angels themselves. (10) Either all these arguments are to be discarded, so that divinity may not be asserted of Christ, or if these arguments cannot be refuted, let the heretics give back to Christ His own divinity.

Chapter 17

What would you reply if I should say that Moses follows this same Rule of Truth and has given us enough in the beginning of his writing to teach us that all things are created and founded through the Son of God, that is, through the Word of God? He states what John and the rest affirm. In fact, John and the others are known to have received from Him what they assert. (2) For John says, "All things were made through Him and nothing was made without

7 Cf. Deut. 4.2; 13.1; Rev. 22.18-19.
8 John 1.3.

Him,"[1] and the Prophet says, "I speak of my works to the king,"[2] and Moses represents God as commanding first that there be light, then that the heavens be firmly established, the waters be gathered together, the dry land appear, fruit come forth according to its seed, animals be produced, the luminaries and stars be set in the heavens.[3] He thus makes it clear that no one else was then present with God, on whom could be enjoined the task of executing these works, save Him through whom "all things were made, and without whom nothing was made."[4] (3) And as He is the Word of God ("My heart has uttered a good word"),[5] he shows that the Word was in the beginning, that this Word was with the Father, and that the Word was God, all things were made through Him. Furthermore, this "Word was made flesh and dwelt among us,"[6] namely, Christ, the Son of God. We acknowledge Him to be later Man according to the flesh, just as we know that He was the Word of God and God before the creation of the world. Consequently, we believe and hold, according to the teaching of the Old and the New Testaments, that Christ Jesus is both God and Man.

(4) Again, what would you reply, if I should say that Moses introduces God as saying; "Let us make man to our image and likeness";[7] and further on, "and God made man, to the image of God He made him, male and female He made them"?[8] If, as we have already shown, it is the Son of God through whom all things were made, then assuredly, it is the Son of God through whom man—for whose sake all things were made—was also created. (5) When God commands that man be made, He who makes man is said to be God; however, it is the Son of God, namely, the Word of God, "through whom all things were made and without whom nothing was made,[9]

1 John 1.3.
2 Ps. 44.2.
3 Cf. Gen. 1.3 ff.
4 John 1.3.
5 Ps. 44(45).2.
6 John 1.14.
7 Gen. 1.26.
8 Gen. 1.27.
9 John 1.3.

who makes man. Furthermore, this "Word was made Flesh and dwelt among us";[10] therefore Christ is God. Accordingly, man was made through Christ, through the Son of God. If God made man to the image of God, then He who made man to the image of God must be God. Therefore Christ is God. Consequently, the authority of the Old Testament regarding the Person of Christ remains unshaken because it is supported by the testimony of the New Testament.[11] Nor is the force of the New Testament undermined, since its truth has under it the roots of this same Old Testament. (6) They who take it for granted that Christ, the Son of God and the Son of Man, is only man and not also God are really acting contrary to both the Old and the New Testament, inasmuch as they are destroying the authority and the truth of both the Old and the New Testaments.

(7) Finally, what would you reply if I should say that the same Moses everywhere represents God the Father as boundless, without end? He cannot be confined by space, for He includes all space. He is not in one place, but rather all place is in Him. He contains all things and embraces all things; therefore He cannot descend or ascend inasmuch as He contains all things and fills all things. Yet Moses represents God as descending to the tower which the sons of men were building, seeking to inspect it and saying: "Come, let us go down quickly, and there confuse their language, so that they may not understand one another's speech."[12] Who do the heretics think was the God that descended to the tower in this passage, and then sought to visit these men? Was He God the Father? In that case, God is enclosed in a place; how then does He embrace all things? (8) Or is it possible that he speaks of an angel descending with other angels and saying: "Come, and let us go down quickly, and confuse their language"? On the contrary, we note in Deuteronomy that it was God who recounted these things and God who spoke, where it is written: "When He scattered abroad the sons of Adam, He set up the boundaries of the people according to the number of the angels of

10 John 1.14.
11 Cf. Augustine, *Quaestionum* 73 *in Exodum* (CCL 33.106; PL 34.623); *De catechizandis rudibus* 4.8 (tr. by J. P. Christopher, ACW 2.23).
12 Gen. 11.7.

God."[13] Therefore the Father did not descend, nor did an angel command these things, as the facts clearly indicate. (9) Accordingly, the only remaining conclusion is that He descended of whom the apostle Paul says: "He who descended, He it is who ascended also above all the heavens, that He might fill all things,"[14] that is, the Son of God, the Word of God. But "the Word was made flesh and dwelt among us."[15] This must be Christ. Therefore we must affirm that Christ is God.

Chapter 18

Please note that the same Moses says in another passage that God appeared to Abraham.[1] Yet the same Moses hears from God that no man can see God and live.[2] If God cannot be seen, how did God appear? If He appeared, how is it that He cannot be seen? (2) For John says in like manner: "No one has ever seen God."[3] And the apostle Paul says: "Whom no man has seen or can see."[4] But certainly, Scripture does not lie; therefore, God was really seen. Accordingly, this can only mean that it was not the Father, who never has been seen, that was seen, but the Son, who is wont both to descend and to be seen, for the simple reason that He has descended. (3) In fact, He is "the image of the invisible God,"[5] that our limited human nature and frailty might in time grow accustomed to see God the Father in Him who is the Image of God, that is, in the Son of God. Gradually and by degrees human frailty had to be strengthened by means of the Image for the glory of being able one day to see God the Father. (4) Great things are dangerous if they

13 Deut 32.8. Novatian sees in the expression "scattered abroad" an allusion to the dispersion at the tower of Babel.
14 Eph. 4.10.
15 John 1.14.

1 Cf. Gen. 12.7; 18.1.
2 Exod. 33.20.
3 John 1.18; 1 John 4.12.
4 1 Tim. 6.16.
5 Col. 1.15.

happen suddenly. Even the light of the sun, striking suddenly with excessive brilliance upon eyes accustomed to the darkness, will not manifest the light of day but rather will cause blindness. Therefore, so that our human eyes may not suffer much injury, the darkness is gradually dispersed and driven away, and that luminary stealthily shows itself by rising little by little. Thus men's eyes are slowly accustomed, by the gradual intensification of its rays, to bear its full orb. (5) In like manner Christ, the image of God and the very Son of God, was presented to the eyes of men only insofar as He was able to be seen. Thus the frailty and weakness of man's present condition is sustained, assisted, and fostered by Him, so that in time, by being accustomed to behold the Son, it may be able to see God the Father Himself as He is. Otherwise, human frailty would succumb to the sudden and unbearable brightness of God's majesty, and would be so overwhelmed that it could not possibly see God the Father, whom it has always desired to see. (6) Therefore, it is the Son who is seen here. But the Son of God is the Word of God: "The Word" of God "was made flesh and dwelt among us";[6] and He is Christ. What in the world is the reason we hesitate to call Him God, when we have so many proofs that He is God?

(7) When Hagar, Sarah's maidservant, had been banished, from her home and put to flight, she was met at a spring of water on the road to Shur by an angel, who questioned her and learned the reason for her flight. She was advised to humble herself, with the hope that she would later bear the title of mother. Furthermore, the angel vowed and promised that the progeny of her womb would be numerous. Not only was Ishmael to be born of her but the angel also made known to her, among other things, the place of Ishmael's abode and described his manner of life.[7] Now Scripture portrays this angel as both Lord and God, for He would not have promised the blessing of progeny if He had not been both angel and God. Let the heretics try to explain away this passage. (8) Was it the Father who was seen by Hagar, or not? For it was stated that He was God. Far be it from

6 John 1.14.
7 Gen. 16.7-12.

us to call God the Father an angel, lest He be subject to another, whose angel He would be. (9) But they will say that He was an angel. If He was an angel, how could He possibly be God since this name has never been given to angels? However, if we examine both sides of the question, truth itself drives us to this conclusion: we must acknowledge that He was the Son of God. Because He is of God, He is rightly called God, since He is the Son of God; and because He is subject to the Father and herald of the Father's will, he is proclaimed "Angel of Great Counsel."[8] (10) Therefore, if this passage is not appropriate to the person of the Father, lest He be called an angel, nor to the person of an angel, lest He be called God, it does, however, suit the person of Christ, since He is not only God, inasmuch as He is the Son of God, but also an angel, inasmuch as He is the herald of the Father's dispensation.[9] Heretics must realize that they are acting contrary to the Scriptures when they say they believe that Christ was also an angel, but do not want to admit that He is also the God who they read came frequently to visit the human race in the Old Testament.

(11) Moses also added that God appeared to Abraham "at the oak of Mamre, as he was sitting at the entrance of his tent at midday,"[10] and though he saw three men, he addressed only one of them as Lord. When he had washed their feet and offered them bread baked on ashes with butter and an abundance of milk, he pleaded with them to remain as his guests and dine. (12) Later, he hears from them that he will be a father and learns that Sarah, his wife, will bear him a son.[11] He is informed of the destruction of the Sodomites and what they deserved to suffer. Finally, he learns that God has come down because of the ill repute of the Sodomites.[12] (13) If in

8 Isa. 9.6(5). This title found its way into the Christian liturgies—e.g, into the Roman rite as part of the introit for the third Mass of Christmas.
9 The argument is that Christ is both God and angel, a title which becomes only the Son of God. Cf. Hilary of Poitiers, *The Trinity* (tr. by S. McKenna, FC 25.1954) pp. 111-22, 143-45, 534. Novatian argues from the original meaning of *angelus* in Greek—that of "messenger," "announcer."
10 Gen. 18.1.
11 Cf. Gen. 18.2-10.
12 Cf. Gen. 18.16-32.

this passage the heretics are of the opinion that it was the Father
who was hospitably received at that time with the two angels, then
the heretics believe that the Father is visible. If they say that it was
an angel, then why is an angel addressed with the unusual title of
God, since one of the three angels was called Lord? The only possible explanation that will render to God the Father His proper in-
visibility and to an angel His proper inferior position is to believe
that no one but the Son of God, who is also God, was seen and
hospitably received by Abraham. (14) As Abraham's guest, He was
prefiguring in a mystery what He would one day be, when He would
find Himself among the sons of Abraham. For He washed their
feet [13] to prove that it was really He; thus, He repaid Abraham's sons
their claim to hospitality which their father had previously extended
to Him. (15) And that there might not remain any doubt that He
had been the guest of Abraham, it is written regarding the destruction of the Sodomites: "When the Lord poured down on Sodom and
Gomorrah fire and sulphur from the Lord out of heaven." [14] In fact,
the prophet also says in the person of God: "I destroyed you, as the
Lord destroyed Sodom and Gomorrah." [15] (16) The Lord, therefore,
destroyed Sodom; that is, God destroyed Sodom. In the destruction
of the Sodomites, however, it was the Lord who rained fire from the
Lord. This Lord was the God seen by Abraham. [16] This God is
Abraham's guest [17] and was undoubtedly seen because He was touched. Now, since the Father, inasmuch as He is invisible, was assuredly
not seen at that time, He who was seen and who was hospitably
received and taken in was He who was wont to be seen and touched.
This one then is the Son of God, "the Lord, who rained upon
Sodom and Gomorrah fire and sulphur from the Lord." [18] But He is
the Word of God: and the "Word" of God "was made flesh, and
dwelt among us." [19] This one then is Christ. (17) Therefore, it was

13 Cf. John 13.5.
14 Gen. 19.24. Cf. Tertullian, *Adv. Prax.* 13; Irenaeus, *Adv. haer.* 3.6.
15 Amos 4.11.
16 Cf. Gen. 12.7; 18.1.
17 Cf. Gen. 18.3-8.
18 Gen. 19.24.
19 John 1.14.

not the Father who was the guest of Abraham but Christ. Nor was it
the Father who was seen, but the Son; therefore, it was Christ who
was seen. Consequently, Christ is both Lord and God, who could be
seen by Abraham only because He was God, the Word, begotten of
God the Father before Abraham even existed.[20]

(18) Furthermore, Moses relates that this same angel, who is also
God, visited and consoled Hagar when she fled from Abraham's home
with her son. For when she had abandoned the child in the desert
because there was no more water in the bottle and when the boy
cried out, she mourned and wept aloud.[21] "And God," says Scripture, "heard the voice of the boy from the place where he was."[22]
(19) When Scripture had recounted that it was God who had heard
the child's voice, Scripture added: "And the angel of the Lord called
to Hagar from heaven."[23] Scripture calls Him an angel whom it has
just called God and declares that He is Lord whom it had just represented as an angel. And He, being angel and God, promises Hagar
even greater consolations, saying: "Do not fear, for I have heard the
voice of the boy from the place where he was. Arise, take up the boy
and hold him, for I will make him a great nation."[24] (20) Why does
this angel, if he be only an angel, claim for himself the right to say:
"For I will make him a great nation,"[25] since this kind of power
undoubtedly belongs to God and cannot belong to an angel? Consequently, it proves that He who can do this is also God. To prove
this very point, Scripture immediately adds: "And God opened her
eyes, and she saw a well of spring water, and she went and filled the
bottle with water and gave the boy a drink, and God was with the
child."[26] (21) Therefore He, who was with the child and opened the
eyes of Hagar so that she might see the well of spring water and draw
water to satisfy the child's urgent need of a drink, was God. On the
other hand, if He who called to her from Heaven was God, then we

20 Cf. John 8.58.
21 Cf. Gen. 21.14-20.
22 Gen 21.17.
23 *Ibid.*
24 Gen. 21.17-18.
25 Gen. 21.18.
26 Gen. 21.19-20.

must realize that He who was called an angel is really not only an angel but God as well—even though earlier in the narrative, when He heard the cry of the boy, He was simply called God. (22) Now, although all this cannot be appropriately and suitably applied to the Father, who is only God, it can, however, be appropriately applied to Christ who has been proclaimed not only God but an angel also. It is quite evident, then, that it was not the Father who spoke to Hagar in the present passage but rather Christ, because He is God. The title of angel is also appropriate to Christ because He was made "the Angel of Great Counsel."[27] He is an angel because He lays bare the heart of the Father,[28] as John declares. (23) For if John says that this Word, who lays bare the bosom of the Father, was also made flesh,[29] so that He could lay bare the heart of the Father, it follows that Christ is not only man but also an angel. And the Scriptures show not only that He is an angel but also that He is God. This is what we too believe. For, if we will not admit that it was Christ who then spoke to Hagar, we must either make an angel God or reckon God the Almighty Father among the angels.

Chapter 19

What will you reply if in another passage we read also that God was described as an angel? In fact, when Jacob was complaining to his wives, Leah and Rachel, of the injustice of their father and when he told them that now he desired to go and return to his native land, he pleaded on the authority of a dream of his and related that an angel of God had said to him in a dream:[1] " 'Jacob, Jacob.' And I," he continues, "said, 'What is it?' And he said, 'Lift up your eyes, and take note: the he-goats and rams are mating with the she-goats and the sheep, and are streaked with white, of divers colors, grizzled and speckled. For I have seen all that Laban has done to you. I am the God who appeared to you in the place of God, where you

27 Isa. 9.6(5).
28 Cf. John 1.18.
29 Cf. John 1.14.
---
1 Cf. Gen. 31.4-11.

anointed the memorial pillar in my behalf and made a vow to me. Now therefore arise, depart from this land, and go to the land of your birth and I shall be with you' "[2] (2) If the angel of God speaks these things to Jacob and the angel himself goes on to say: "I am the God who appeared to you in the place of God,"[3] we immediately perceive that He is declared to be not only an angel but also God, since He says that Jacob's vow was made to Him "in the place of God,"[4] and does not say, "in my place." It is therefore the place of God, and He who speaks is also God. (3) Furthermore, it is simply written: "in the place of God,"[5] not "in the place of the angel and of God," but only "of God." Now He who promises these things is said to be God and angel. Consequently, there must be a distinction between Him who is called simply God and Him who is declared to be not simply God, but an angel as well. (4) Accordingly, if there is no other angel, whose authority can here be judged so great that he can claim to be God and attest that a vow had been made to him, except Christ alone—to whom a vow can be made not as to a mere angel but as to God—then it is quite evident that He cannot be regarded as the Father, but the Son who is both God and angel. (5) If He is Christ—as indeed He is—that man is in great danger who says that Christ is only a man or only an angel and denies Him the power due His Holy Name, a power He has frequently received according to the authority of the heavenly Scriptures,[6] which repeatedly call Him both God and angel.

(6) To all these considerations, we can add that, just as divine Scripture repeatedly asserts that Christ is God and angel, so too does the same divine Scripture assert that He is both God and Man, when it explains what He was to be and represents in a figure, even at that early period, what nature He was to have in very substance. (7) Scripture recounts "Jacob remained alone; and a man wrestled with

2 Gen. 31.11-13.
3 Gen. 31.13.
4 *Ibid.*
5 *Ibid.*
6 For Novatian Holy Scripture is: (1) "divine" (chs. 19.6, 24.6, 26.1); (2) "holy" (ch. 30.7); (3) "heavenly" (chs. 6.1, 19.5, 21.1, 23.6, 24.6, 30.16, 19).

him until the break of day. And he saw that he could not prevail
against him, and he touched the broad part of Jacob's thigh while he
struggled against him, and he with him, and he said to him, 'Let me
go, for the morning star is rising.' And he said, 'I will not let you
go, unless you bless me.' And he said, 'What is your name?'
And he said, 'Jacob.' And he said to him, 'Your name shall not be
called Jacob any longer, but Israel shall be your name; for you have
prevailed with God, and with men you are powerful.' "[7] Furthermore, Scripture adds: "And Jacob called the name of that place
Vision of God; for 'I have seen God face to face, and my life has
been spared.' And the sun rose upon him and soon he passed the
Vision of God; but he limped because of his thigh."[8] (8) A man,
Scripture says, wrestled with Jacob. If he is a mere man, who is he?
Where did he come from? Why does he struggle and wrestle with
Jacob? What had come between them? What had happened? What
was the cause of so great a conflict and struggle as that? Moreover,
why is it that Jacob proves to be the stronger even to the holding of
the man with whom he was struggling? And why still, because the
morning star was rising, is it he who, on that account, asks a blessing
from him whom he held? It can only mean that this struggle was
prefiguring that future contention between Christ and the sons of
Jacob, which is said to have had its completion in the Gospel. (9)
For Jacob's people struggled against this man and proved to be more
powerful in the conflict, because they obtained the triumph of their
own unrighteousness over Christ. Then, on account of the crime
they had perpetrated, they began to limp very badly in the gait of
their own faith and salvation, stumbling and slipping in their course.
Though Jacob's people proved superior by their condemnation of
Christ, they still need His mercy and still need His blessing. (10)
Now, this man who wrestled with Jacob says to him, "Your name
shall no longer be called Jacob, but Israel shall be your name."[9]
And if Israel is a man who 'sees God,' then the Lord was showing in
an elegant manner that he who wrestled with Jacob was not only

7 Gen. 32.25-28.
8 Gen. 32.31-32.
9 Gen. 32.28-29.

man, but also God. (11) Undoubtedly, Jacob saw God with whom he wrestled, though it was a man whom he held in his grip. That there might not remain any doubt, he himself gave the interpretation when he said: "For you have prevailed with God, and with men you are powerful." [10] (12) That is why this same Jacob, understanding now the meaning of the prefiguration and realizing the authority of him with whom he had wrestled, called the name of the place where he had wrestled "Vision of God." (13) Furthermore, he added his reasons for giving his interpretation of God: "I have seen God face to face, and my soul has been saved." [11] For he saw God with whom he wrestled, as though he were wrestling with a man; but while as if victor he held the man, as an inferior [12] he asked a blessing of him, as one would of God. Thus he wrestled with God and with man. (14) Now if this struggle was then prefigured and has been actually fulfilled in the Gospel between Christ and Jacob's people—a struggle in which the people proved superior, yet were found to be inferior because of their guilt—who will hesitate to acknowledge that Christ in whom this figure of a struggle was fulfilled was not only Man but also God, when that very figure of a struggle seems to have proved that He is both God and Man?

(15) And yet, even after all these arguments, Scripture rightly does not cease to call an angel God, and God an angel. (16) When this same Jacob was about to bless Manasseh and Ephraim, the sons of Joseph, he placed his hands crosswise upon the heads of the boys [13] and said: "May God who has nourished me from my youth even to this day, the angel who has delivered me from all evils, bless the boys." [14] (17) So conclusively does he affirm that the same one whom he had called God is an angel that he does not hesitate towards the end of his sentence to place the person of whom he was speaking in the singular number, saying: "May He bless these boys." [15] (18) For if he had meant the angel to be taken as a separate person, he would have

10 *Ibid.*
11 Gen. 32.31.
12 Cf. Heb. 7.7.
13 Cf. Gen. 48.14.
14 Gen. 48.15-16.
15 *Ibid.*

joined two persons together in the plural number; instead he used the singular number for one person in the blessing. Consequently, he wished the same person to be considered God and angel. (19) Although God the Father cannot be considered to be an angel, Christ can readily be taken to be both God and angel. By laying his hands crosswise on the heads of the boys,[16] Jacob designated Christ as the author of this blessing, implying that Christ was their father. Accordingly, by the way in which he placed his hands, he was manifesting a figure and a future symbol of the Passion. (20) Just as no one hesitates to call Christ an angel, so too let no one hesitate to call Him also God, especially when he sees that He was invoked as both God and angel in the blessing of the boys through the mystery of His Passion, shown forth in the figure of the crossed hands.

Chapter 20

If any heretic obstinately resisting the truth would want to imply or even insist that an angel in the proper sense of the word must be understood in all these instances, he must also be defeated in this stand of his by the forces of truth. (2) Now if all things, celestial, terrestrial, and infernal, which have been subjected to Christ,[1] even the very angels, with all possible creatures subject to Christ, are called gods,[2] then rightly Christ also is God. And yet any angel subject to Christ can be called god; furthermore, if this is said, it can even be said without blasphemy. Hence, it is indeed much more fitting that Christ, the very Son of God, should be proclaimed God. (3) For if an angel, who is subject to Christ, is declared to be a god, much more and more fittingly will Christ, to whom all angels are subject, be said to be God. In fact, it is not in accord with natural propriety to deny to the greater what has been granted to the lesser. So if an angel who is less than Christ, is, nevertheless, called a god, it

---

16 Cf. Gen. 48.14.

1 Cf. Matt. 28.18; Eph. 1.20-22; 1 Peter 3.22.
2 Cf. Ps. 81(82).6 (?). Only here in Sacred Scripture are angels called gods. Novatian argues as follows: All things, angels included, are subject to Christ. An angel, however, may be called a god; *a fortiori,* then, is Christ rightly called God.

follows quite readily that Christ, who is both greater and better than not just one angel but all of them, is to be called God. (4) Now if "God stood in the assembly of the gods and in their midst God judges the gods,"[3] and Christ stood several times in the assembly, then Christ stood in the assembly as God judging the gods, to whom He says: "How long do you respect the persons of men? "[4] He thereby accused the men of the assembly of judging unjustly. (5) Furthermore, if they who are reproved and blamed seem for some reason or other to acquire this name without blasphemy, so that they can be called gods, much more, assuredly, shall He be regarded as God who is said not only to have stood as the God of gods, but to have been revealed to us by the authority of the same passage, as judging and passing sentence on gods. (6) Now if they who "fall like one of the princes"[5] are, nevertheless, called gods, much more shall He be called God who not only does not fall as one of the princes, but even overcomes the very author and prince of wickedness. (7) Why in the world, after reading that this name was also given to Moses, when it is stated: "I have made you as God to Pharaoh,"[6] should they deny this title to Christ who we find has been constituted not a god to Pharaoh, but rather the Lord and God of all creation? (8) And in the former case the name is given with a qualification in the latter unreservedly; in the former case, by measure, in the latter, beyond all measure whatever ("for the Father," says Scripture, "does not give by measure to the Son, for the Father loves the Son");[7] in the former case, for a time; in the latter, without reference to time. In fact, Christ received the power of the Divine Name, not only over all things but for all time. (9) Now

3 Ps. 81(82).1.

4 Ps. 81(82).2.

5 Ps. 81(82).7. The older commentators (Novatian, Eusebius of Caesarea, Theodoret, Origen, Hesychius, Augustine, and others) refer the expression "one of the princes" to Satan. Modern commentators, however, think that it means simply "like any prince."

6 Exod. 7.1.

7 John 3.34-35. Just as man in loving God must love Him without measure (St. Bernard, *On the Love of God* 1.1, 6.16), so God Himself loves without measure.

if he who received power over one man, notwithstanding the limited power given him, is without hesitation granted the name of God, how much more shall we believe that He who has power even over Moses has received the authority of the name given to Him?

Chapter 21

I could have very well sifted through the statements of all the Heavenly Scriptures and, if I may use the expression, produced a veritable forest of texts on this question of Christ's divinity. However, I did not intend to speak against this particular heresy, but rather to explain briefly the Rule of Truth regarding the person of Christ. (2) Although I must hasten on to other matters, I do not think that I ought to omit what the Lord expressed in the Gospel as a mysterious indication of His majesty, when He said: "Destroy this temple, and in three days I will raise it up"[1] or when He stated in another place, and in a different context: "I have power to lay down My life and take it up again, for I have received this command from the Father."[2] (3) Now, who is this who says that He has power to lay down His life or that He can restore His life again, because He has received this command from the Father? Or who says that He can raise up again and rebuild the ruined temple of His body? He can be no other than the Word who is of the Father, who is with the Father,[3] through whom "all things were made, and without whom nothing was made."[4] He is the imitator of the Father's works and mighty deeds,[5] the "image of the invisible God,"[6] who "came down from heaven,"[7] who "bore witness to that which He has seen and heard,"[8] who did not come to do His own Will but rather to do the Will of the Father,[9] by whom He had been sent for this very pur-

1 John 2.19.
2 John 10.18.
3 John 1.1-2.
4 John 1.3.
5 Cf. John 5.19.
6 Col. 1.15.
7 John 3.31.
8 John 3.32.
9 Cf. John 6.38-39.

pose. He was constituted the "Angel of Great Counsel"[10] that He might reveal to us the laws of heavenly mysteries. He, the Word made flesh, dwelt among us.[11] He, therefore, is this Christ who, as one of us, has been clearly demonstrated to be not only Man inasmuch as He is the Son of Man, but also God because He is the Son of God.

(4) Now, if Christ is called by the Apostle "the firstborn of all creatures,"[12] how could He be the firstborn of all creatures unless—in virtue of His divinity—He came forth, as the Word from the Father before every creature? But if the heretics do not interpret the above passage in this manner, they will be compelled to prove that Christ, as man, is the firstborn of all creatures, something they have not been able to do. (5) Therefore, either He is before every creature, so as to be the firstborn of all creatures (then He is not merely a man because man is after every created thing) or else He is merely a man and consequently after every created thing. (6) And how is He the firstborn of all creatures, if not by virtue of His being that divine Word that is before every creature? Therefore, the firstborn of all creatures is made flesh and dwells among us—that is, He assumes this humanity which is after all creation—and thus, with it and in it, dwells among us, so that neither is humanity taken away from Christ nor is divinity denied Him. (7) For if He is merely before every creature, humanity is taken away from Him. On the other hand, if He is only man, His divinity, which is before every creature, is done away with. Both then are united in Christ, both are conjoined, both are linked together. (8) This is rightly so, since there is something in Him that surpasses every creature, inasmuch as the union of the divinity and the humanity seems to be secured in Him. For this reason, He who is declared to have been made "the Mediator between God and man"[13] is found to have associated in Himself both God and Man.

(9) And when the same Apostle says of Christ: "He, having put off

10 Isa. 9.6.
11 John 1.14.
12 Col. 1.15.
13 1 Tim. 2.5.

the flesh, dishonored the Powers, openly triumphing over them in Himself," [14] certainly he did not intend that the phrase, "having put off the flesh," should have no meaning at all. On the contrary, he intended it to mean that He put on the flesh again in His Resurrection. (10) Let the heretics, then, find out for themselves who it is that puts off and again puts on the flesh. For we know that it was the Word of God who put on the substance of flesh and that this selfsame Word divested Himself of the very same material of His body, which he took again in His Resurrection, and put on anew, as though it were a garment. (11) If Christ had been only a man, He could neither have divested Himself of nor clothed Himself with humanity since no one is ever divested of or clothed with himself. Whatever is taken way from or put on by someone must of necessity be something other than the person himself. (12) Consequently, it was assuredly the Word of God who put off the flesh and in His Resurrection put it on again. He discarded it because He had put it on in His Nativity. So in Christ it is God who is clothed, and it must also be God who was divested because He who is clothed must likewise be divested. He, then, puts on and puts off humanity, as though His body were a woven tunic. Therefore it was the Word of God, as we have already stated, who is found to have at one time put on and at another time to have put off the flesh. (13) He even foretold this in the blessing: "He shall wash His garment in wine, and His clothing in the blood of the grape." [15] (14) If in Christ the garment is His flesh and the clothing His body, then one may ask, who it is whose body is His clothing and His flesh His garment. It is quite evident to us that the flesh was the garment and the body was the clothing of the Word who washed the substance of His body and the matter of His flesh in the blood, that is, in wine, cleansing by His

14 Col. 2.15; cf. Hilary, *De Trin.* 1.13 (tr. McKenna, FC 25.13-14). The literal meaning of the text is that God despoiled or disarmed the vile angels (Principalities and Powers) of their power by His death on the Cross. Novatian and, in general, the Latin Fathers interpret the passage to mean "Christ stripped Himself of His body" by His death on the Cross and clothed Himself with humanity again when He arose from the dead.
15 Gen. 49.11. Verses 1-27 of this chapter sometimes carry the heading "Jacob's *Blessings*"; here Jacob foretells the future of his sons. Verse 11 relates to Judah.

Passion that humanity He had taken upon Himself.[16] (15) Therefore, inasmuch as He is washed, He is man, because the garment that is washed is flesh; but He who washes it is the Word of God, who, in order to wash the garment, was made the wearer of the garment. (16) Accordingly, He is declared to be Man by that substance which was assumed that it might be washed, just as He who washed it is shown to be God, by the authority of the Word.

Chapter 22

Although we find ourselves hurrying on to another part of the discussion, we cannot omit that well-known passage of the Apostle: "Who though He was in the form of God, thought it not robbery to be equal to God, but emptied Himself, taking the form of a slave, being made in the likeness of men, and in habit found as a man. He humbled Himself, becoming obedient even to death, the death of the Cross. Therefore God also has exalted Him exceedingly, and has bestowed upon Him the name that is above every name; so that at the name of Jesus every knee should bend of those in heaven, on earth and under the earth, and every tongue should confess that the Lord Jesus is in the glory of God the Father."[1] (2) The Apostle says: "Who though He was in the form of God."[2] If Christ, then, were only man, He would have been referred to as in the image of God, not as in the form of God. For we know that man was made to the image, not according to the form of God.[3] (3) Who, then, is this, who was made, as we have said, in the form of God? An angel? But nowhere in Scripture do we read about angels in the form of God, simply because He alone is the first and of noble birth before all others: the Son of God, the Word of God, the Imitator of all His Father's works.[4] Inasmuch as He also works as His Father does,[5] He is, as we have said, in the form of God the Father. (4) Rightly, then,

---

16 Cf. Hippolytus, *De antichristo* 11; Tertullian, *Adv. Marc.* 4.40.

1 Phil. 2.6-11.
2 Phil. 2.6.
3 Gen. 1.26-27.
4 Cf. John 5.19.
5 John 5.17.

has He been declared to be in the form of God, because He is above all things, holds divine authority over every creature, and is God after the likeness of His Father. However, He received this from His own Father, that He might be both God and Lord of all and God according to the form of God the Father, begotten and brought forth from Him. (5) Therefore, though "He was in the form of God, He did not think it robbery to be equal to God."[6] For though He was ever mindful that He was God of God the Father, He never compared or ranked Himself with God the Father, knowing that He is of His Father; and this very thing (that He is) He had, because the Father had given it to Him. Hence, not only before He took upon Himself the flesh but even after He had taken a body, and again, after His Resurrection, He rendered and still renders perfect obedience to His Father in all things. (6) Consequently, this proves that He never regarded His divinity as a means of unlawfully arrogating to Himself equality with God the Father. On the contrary, obedient and subject to His Father's every command and will, He was even content to take upon Himself the form of a slave—that is, to become man.[7] He took upon Himself by His birth the substance of flesh and of the body which fell to His lot from the bondage incurred by the transgressions of His forefathers and according to His human nature.

At that time, He also emptied Himself, for He did not refuse to take upon Himself the human frailty of human existence. (7) Had he been born a mere man, He would never, because of that, have been emptied. Man, by being born, is not emptied but rather acquires something. When he begins to be, he acquires what he could not have had when He did not exist; as a result, he is not emptied, as we have said, but rather acquires and is enriched. (8) And if Christ is emptied, since He is born, taking the form of a slave, how, then, is He merely a man? Of Christ it would have been more correct to say that He was enriched when He was born, not emptied, for the simple

6 Phil. 2.6.
7 Christ is sinless, but by His Incarnation He became part of a sinful race and bore the burden of our sins.

reason that the majesty of the Divine Word, condescending for the moment to take upon itself humanity and not exercising itself in its powers, lowers and abases itself for a time, while bearing the humanity that it has taken upon itself. (9) He empties Himself when He condescends to affronts and insults, when He hears blasphemies and suffers unbecoming things.

His abasement, however, bears excellent fruit, (10) since He received a "name which is above every name,"[8] which name indeed we know can only be the name of God. In fact, since God alone is above all things, it follows that that name is above all things, which belongs to Him who is above all things, namely God. It is therefore, that name which is above every name, which name consequently must assuredly belong to Him who, though he had been in the form of God, thought it not robbery to be equal to God. (11) For if Christ were not also God, every knee of those in heaven, on earth, and under the earth would not bend at His name.[9] Neither things visible nor those invisible, nor creation itself would be subject and subservient to a man, since they would be mindful of the fact that they existed before man. (12) Christ, then, is said to be in the form of God. He is shown to have emptied Himself in His Nativity according to the flesh.[10] He is said to have received from His Father a name that is above every name. It is clear to all that every knee of those in heaven, on earth, and under the earth bends and bows at His name; furthermore, it is stated that this redounds to the glory of God the Father.[11] Consequently, the fact that He "became obedient" to the Father "unto death, even to the death of the cross"[12] does not mean that He is only man. On the contrary, if we consider the foregoing proofs which loudly proclaim Christ's divinity, we find that the Lord Christ Jesus proves to be also God. The heretics do not accept this truth.

8 Phil. 2.9.
9 Cf. Phil. 2.10.
10 Cf. Phil. 2.6-7.
11 Cf. Phil. 2.9-11.
12 Phil. 2.8.

Chapter 23

In this chapter I will permit myself the liberty of marshaling my arguments even from the point of view of other heretics. It is indeed a very efficacious kind of proof that is taken even from one's adversary to demonstrate the truth by means of the very enemies of truth.[1] (2) The Scriptures so clearly teach that Christ is also God that many heretics,[2] deeply moved by the reality and the grandeur of His divinity, stressed His glories to such an extent that they did not hesitate to declare (or at least were of the opinion) that He was not the Son, but God the Father Himself. (3) Though this opinion of theirs is contrary to the truth of the Scriptures, it is, nevertheless, a weighty and excellent argument for the divinity of Christ. He is so indisputably God—that is, as Son of God, born of God—that many heretics, as we have said, took Him to be God in such a manner that they thought that He must be called the Father, not the Son. (4) Let the heretics, then, decide whether He is God or not, bearing in mind, however, that His divine majesty has so greatly moved certain people that, as we stated above, they already were of the opinion that He was indeed God the Father Himself. They acknowledge, without due moderation and restraint, the divinity in Christ because they are compelled to do so by Christ's incontestable divinity. Hence, though they read in Scripture that He is the Son, they think that He is the Father because they readily perceive that the Son is God. (5) Other heretics[3] cling with such tenacity to the evident divinity of Christ that they say He was without flesh. Thus, they have stripped Him entirely of the humanity He took upon Himself, because they thought that they would reduce the power of the divine name in Him if they were to associate, in any way, a human birth with Him. (6) We do not approve of this; nevertheless, we can use it as an argument to prove that Christ is so indisputably God that some heretics have done away with His humanity and think that He is only

---

1 Cf. Eusebius, *Historia ecclesiastica* 7.
2 The Sabellians, already referred to in ch. 12.
3 Namely, those attacked by Tertullian in *De carne Christi.*

God, while others believe that He is God the Father Himself. Since reason and the harmony existing between the various parts of the Heavenly Scriptures show that Christ is God–but as the Son of God–and since the Son of Man has been assumed by God, we must believe that He is also Man. (7) For if He was coming to man so that He might be "the Mediator between God and man,"[4] He had to be with man. The Word had to become flesh[5] that He might unite in Himself the alliance between earthly and heavenly things by incorporating the pledges of both parties in Himself, thus uniting God with man and man with God.[6] Accordingly, the Son of God could become the Son of Man by taking flesh, and the Son of Man could become the Son of God by the reception of the Word of God. (8) This most profound and recondite mystery,[7] destined for the salvation of the human race before the ages,[8] had its fulfillment in the Lord Jesus Christ, who is God and Man, so that the human race might be brought through Him to the enjoyment of eternal salvation.

Chapter 24

Now the origin of the heretics' error, I believe, is that they do not think there is a distinction between the Son of God and the Son of Man. For if a distinction were made, it would not be difficult to prove that Jesus Christ is both Man and God. (2) They would have it appear that one and the self-same man–that is, the Son of Man–is also the Son of God, so that the man and the flesh and that self-same frail bodily substance is said to be the Son of God. Therefore, since no distinction is made between the Son of Man and the Son of God and since they claim that the Son of Man Himself is the Son of God,

4 1 Tim. 2.5.
5 Cf. John 1.14.
6 The idea is that man and God have entered into a mutual engagement, of which the Incarnation is the guarantee.
7 Cf. Eph. 1.9.
8 Cf. 2 Tim. 1.9.

they assert that Christ, as a mere man, is likewise the Son of God.
(3) They are endeavoring to exclude by this argument of theirs the
Scriptural passages: "The Word was made flesh and dwelt among
us,"[1] and "You shall call His name Emmanuel, which is interpreted,
God with us."[2]

(4) They bring forward and allege in support of their argument
what is related in the Gospel according to Luke, by virtue of which
they endeavor to assert not the truth as it really is but only as they
desire it to be: "The Holy Spirit shall come upon thee, and the
power of the Most High shall overshadow thee; therefore also the
holy thing to be born of thee shall be called the Son of God."[3] (5)
If, therefore, reply the heretics, the angel of God says to Mary "that
holy thing which shall be born of thee," then the substance of flesh
and body is from Mary. Hence, the angel declared that this
substance—that is, this holy thing that was born of her—is the Son of
God. The man himself, they say, and that very flesh of His body,
that thing that is said to be holy, is itself the Son of God so that
when Scripture mentions "the holy thing," we should understand it
to mean Christ the man, the Son of Man. When Scripture sets before
us the Son of God, we ought to understand not God, but man.

(6) Divine Scripture, however, uncovers and refutes with ease the
deceits and the stratagems of the heretics. For if the wording were
only as follows: "The Spirit shall come upon thee, and the power of
the Most High shall overshadow thee; therefore that holy thing to be
born of thee shall be called the Son of God," perhaps we would have
had to contend with them in another way. We would have had
to look for other arguments and to select other weapons with
which to overcome their snares and charlatanries. But since Scripture
itself, which abounds in heavenly integrity, exonerates itself from
the calumnies of those heretics, we can readily rely upon what has
been written and without hesitation overcome their errors. (7) In
fact, as we have already explained, Scripture did not state: "therefore that holy thing to be born of thee," but added a conjunction

1 John 1.14.
2 Isa. 7.14; Matt. 1.23.
3 Luke 1.35, a verse echoed through the remainder of the chapter.

and stated: "therefore also that holy thing to be born of thee." So Scripture clearly shows that this holy thing that is born of her—that is, that substance of flesh and body—is not primarily but subsequently and secondarily the Son of God. Primarily, however, the Son of God is the Word of God, incarnate through that Spirit of whom the angel relates, "The spirit shall come upon thee, and the power of the Most High shall overshadow thee."

(8) This is the genuine Son of God, who is of God Himself. Inasmuch as He assumes that holy thing and joins to Himself the Son of Man, He not only seizes Him and draws Him over to Himself but also bestows upon Him and makes Him by His connection and associated permixtion the Son of God, which He was not by nature. Thus, the pre-eminence of that name, "Son of God," resides in the Spirit of the Lord who descended and came; whereas the sequela of that name is to be found in the Son of God and Man. In consequence [of such a union] this Son of Man rightly became the Son of God, although He is not primarily the Son of God. (9) Accordingly, the angel, aware of that arrangement and making known the providential order of the mystery, did not confuse everything so as not to leave any vestige of a distinction. He made that distinction when he announced: "Therefore also that holy thing to be born of thee shall be called the Son of God." For if he had not allotted that partition [of natures] with its due balance but had left it in hazy confusion, he would have undoubtedly given the heretics an opportunity to declare that the Son of Man, as man, is the same Son both of God and Man. (10) However, he explained things in detail and clearly made known the providential order and meaning of so great a mystery when he said: "And that holy thing to be born of thee shall be called the Son of God"; hence he proved that the Son of God descended and took to Himself the Son of Man and made Him, in consequence [of that union], the Son of God. For the Son of God associated and joined the Son of Man to Himself so that, while the Son of Man adheres in His Nativity to the Son of God, by that very permixtion He holds that as pledged and secured which of His own nature He could not possess. (11) And thus by the voice of an angel a distinction which the heretics reject was made between the Son of God and

the Son of Man. This distinction maintains, however, the proper association [of the two] and constrains them to understand that Christ, the Man, the Son of Man, is also the Son of God and to accept as Man the Son of God—that is, the Word of God who is God, according to the Scriptures. Therefore let them acknowledge that Christ Jesus the Lord, fastened together from both, so to speak, woven and worked together from both, and associated in the same agreement of both natures in the clasp of a mutual bond, is God and Man, as the truth of Scripture itself declares.

Chapter 25

Well then, say the heretics, if Christ is not only Man but also God, and Scripture says that Christ died for us and rose again, surely Scripture is teaching us to believe that God died. If God cannot die and Christ is said to have died, Christ cannot be God because God cannot be understood to have died. (2) If they ever could understand or had ever understood what they read, they would undoubtedly have never expressed themselves in such a hazardous manner. But the folly of error is always reckless, and it is not unusual for those who have abandoned the true faith to stoop to foolhardy things. (3) If Scripture had declared that Christ was only God and there was no association of human frailty traceable in Him, then their twisted syllogism would have had some force here: "If Christ is God, and Christ died, then God died." (4) Since Scripture holds Him up to be not only God but also Man, as we have frequently made clear, it follows that what is immortal must be held to have remained uncorrupted. For who does not perceive that the Divinity is incapable of suffering and that human frailty is certainly capable of suffering? (5) Because one readily perceives that in Christ there is a permixtion[1] and association of that which is God and of that which is Man—for "the Word was made flesh and dwelt among us"[2] —who cannot discern by himself, without a teacher or interpreter, that

1 The inconfusion of the two natures in Christ was already most concisely formulated by Tertullian, *Adv. Prax.* 27.
2 John 1.14.

what is God in Christ did not die, but what is Man in Him did die? (6) Why marvel that the divinity of Christ cannot die and that the substance of the flesh alone perishes, when we realize that even in other men, who are not only flesh but flesh and soul, the flesh alone suffers the inroads of dissolution and death; whereas the soul, which is not liable to the laws of dissolution and death, remains obviously uncorrupted? (7) This is what our Lord Himself said when He exhorted us to suffer martyrdom and to despise all human power: "Do not be afraid of those who kill the body but cannot kill the soul."[3] (8) Now if the immortal soul cannot be killed or slain in anyone even though the body and flesh alone can be slain, then how much more, you may be sure, was it absolutely impossible for the Word of God, who is God, to be slain in Christ, when His flesh and body alone were slain. (9) For if the soul in every man possesses this noblesse of immortality, so that it cannot be slain, much more does the noblesse of the Word of God claim this power of not being able to be slain. If the power of men fails to destroy the sacred power of God, and human cruelty fails to slay the soul, much more must it fail to slay the Word of God. If the soul itself, which was created through the Word of God, cannot be slain by men, much more readily should we believe that the Word of God cannot be destroyed. (10) And if man's bloody violence against his fellowman can do no more than kill the body, a fortiori, you can be sure it will be unable to do more than slay, in like manner, only the body of Christ. Therefore we conclude that only the Man in Christ was slain and that it is quite evident that the Word was not thereby subjected to mortality. (11) Certainly it is evident that Abraham, Isaac, and Jacob, who were obviously only men, are alive: "For all these," says the Lord, "live unto"[4] God, and death, which decomposed their bodies, could not destroy their souls. Death could exercise its power over their bodies but could not exercise it over their souls. For we must distinguish in them what was mortal and therefore died, and what was immortal in them and consequently, as we know, could not have been extinguished. Precisely for that reason does Scripture declare and affirm that they live unto God. Now, if this is the case with mere men, then

3 Matt. 10.28.
4 Luke 20.38.

how much more, of course, was death in Christ powerless against the divinity of the Word, even though it was able to prevail against the mere matter of His body. For the power of death is broken where the might of immortality intervenes.

Chapter 26

Since the sacred authority of the Divine Scripture affirms that Christ is not only Man but also God, other heretics[1] use this as a pretext to come forth with a scheme to undermine the very foundation of our devotion to Christ. They want to show that Christ is God the Father by the very fact that He is declared to be not only Man but also God. (2) They express themselves in this manner: Scripture teaches that there is one God. But Christ is God. Therefore, say the heretics, if the Father and Christ are the one God, Christ will be called the Father. In this syllogism they were proved to be in error, not knowing Christ, but rather favoring the mere sound of a name. For they want Him not to be the Second Person after the Father, but the Father Himself. (3) Since we can readily refute them, we shall say just a few words. For who does not acknowledge that the Second Person after the Father is the Son, when he reads what was said by the Father to the Son in view of this relationship: "Let us make men to Our image and likeness";[2] and after these words it is related: "And God made man, according to the image of God He made him"?[3] (4) Or when he holds in his hands the text: "The Lord poured down on Sodom and Gomorrah fire and sulphur from the Lord out of heaven"?[4] (5) Or when he reads [the words addressed] to Christ: "You are my Son; this day I have begotten You. Ask of Me and I will give You the Gentiles for Your inheritance and the ends of the earth for Your possession?"[5] (6) Or when even that

1 The Patripassians.
2 Gen. 1.26.
3 Gen. 1.27.
4 Gen. 19.24.
5 Ps. 2.7-8.

beloved writer says: "The Lord said to My Lord: 'Sit at my right hand till I make your enemies your footstool' "?[6] (7) Or when he opens the prophecies of Isaiah and finds it written: "Thus says the Lord to Christ my Lord"?[7] (8) Or when he reads: "I did not come down from heaven to do My own will, but the will of Him who sent Me"?[8] (9) Or when he finds it written: "For He who sent Me is greater than I"?[9] (10) Or when he considers the passage: "I go to My Father and your Father, to My God and your God"?[10] (11) Or when he finds, among other texts, the statement: "But in your Law it is written that the witness of two persons is true; I bear witness to Myself, and He who sent Me, the Father, bears witness to Me"?[11] (12) Or when a voice from heaven resounds: "I have glorified [it], and I will glorify [it again]"?[12] (13) Or when Peter answered and said: "You are the Son of the living God"?[13] (14) Or when the Lord Himself confirmed the mystery of this revelation, and said: "You are blessed, Simon Bar-Jona, for flesh and blood has not revealed this to you, but My Father who is in heaven"?[14] (15) Or when Christ Himself utters: "Father, glorify Me with the glory that I had with You before the world existed"?[15] (16) Or when the same Christ says: "Father, I knew that You always hear Me; but because of the people who stand round, I spoke, that they may believe that You sent Me"?[16] (17) Or when Christ Himself makes a pronouncement on the Rule [of Truth] and says: "Now this is everlasting life,

6 Ps. 109(110).1.
7 Isa. 45.1.
8 John 6.38.
7 Isa 45.1. Along with many other Greek and Latin writers, Novatian erred by reading in the Greek *kyriōi* ("to the Lord") instead of *kyrōi* ("to Cyrus") and interpreting *christōi* as "Christ" rather than "annointed."
8 John 6.38.
9 John 14.28.
10 John 20.17.
11 John 8.17-18.
12 John 12.28.
13 Matt. 16.16.
14 Matt. 16.17.
15 John 17.5.
16 John 11.42.

that they may know You, the one true God, and Him whom You have sent, Jesus Christ. I have glorified You on earth; I have accomplished the work that You have given Me"? [17] (18) Or again when He asserts and declares: "All things have been delivered to Me by My Father"? [18] (19) Or when both the apostles and the prophets affirm that He sits at the right hand[19] of the Father? (20) Now I should have quite a wearisome task, if I were to try to gather together all the possible passages bearing on this question. For throughout the Divine Scripture of the Old, as well as the New Testament, He is shown to us as born of the Father, one through whom "all things were made, and without whom nothing was made,"[20] who has ever been obedient to the Father and still obeys. He is also revealed to us as having power over all things, power, however, that has been given, that has been granted and conferred upon Him by His own Father. (21) What could make it more evident that He is not the Father but the Son than the fact that He is set before us as obedient to God the Father? If we were to believe otherwise—that He is the Father—then we would have to say that Christ is subject to another God the Father.

Chapter 27

Since the heretics frequently place before us that passage which states: "I am the Father are one [unum],"[1] we shall refute them again with equal facility also on this count. (2) For if Christ were the Father, as the heretics think, He should have said: "I, the Father, am one [unus]." But when He says "I" and then introduces the Father, by saying: "I and the Father," He thereby distinguishes and separates the individuality of His own Person, viz. that of the Son, from the

17 John 17.3-4.
18 Matt. 11.27; Luke 10.22.
19 Cf. Ps. 109(110).1; Mark 16.19; Heb. 1.3.
20 John 1.3.

1 John 10.30. Latin provides three forms of the word for "one" in the nominative case singular: unus (masculine), unum (neuter), and (not here relevant) una (feminine). Novatian's argument in this passage reposes upon this distinction.

authority of the Father, not only as regards the mere sound of the name [Son] but also in regard to the order of power in the divine economy. He could have said: "I the Father," if He were conscious of the fact that He Himself was the Father. (3) Furthermore, since He said "one" [*unum*], let the heretics realize that He did not say "one" [*unus*]. For "one" in the neuter gender denotes harmony of fellowship, not unity of person. He is said to be "one" [*unum*], and not "one" [*unus*], because there is no reference to number but to association of fellowship with another. (4) And in fact He goes on to say "we are," not 'I am," to show that there are two Persons, precisely through saying "We are" and "the Father." When He says "one" [*unum*], He is referring to the harmony, the identity of judgment, the association of love itself existing between them, so that the Father and the Son are rightly one through harmony, through love, and through affection. (5) And because He is of the Father, whatever be the nature of the Father. He is the Son; however, the distinction remains, so that He is not the Father who is the Son, because He is not the Son who is the Father. Nor would He have added "We are," if He had been mindful of the fact that He, the one and only Father, had become the Son.

(6) In fact, the apostle Paul was aware of this harmonious unity along with its corresponding distinction of persons. For he says, in writing to the Corinthians: "I have planted, Apollos watered, but God has given the growth. This means that neither he who plants nor he who waters is of any special account, only God, who gives the growth. Now he who plants and he who waters are one [*unum*]."[2] (7) Who, then, does not see that Apollos is one person, Paul another, and that Apollos and Paul are not equally one and the same person? He declares that the functions of each are distinct: for he who plants is one person, and he who waters is another. The apostle Paul, however, offered these two men for consideration, of the faithful, not because each of them constitutes one [*unus*] individual person but because they are one [*unum*]. Apollos is indeed one person, Paul another, as far as the distinction of persons is concerned; but the

2 1 Cor. 3.6-8.

two are one [*unum*] <with regard to the harmony existing between them>. (8) In fact, when two persons are of one mind, one truth, one faith, of one and the same religion, one also in the fear of God, the two are really one, even though they are two persons. They are the same, inasmuch as they are of the same mind. (9) For those who are separated by reason of personality are brought together again because of religion. Although they are not identically the same persons, yet as long as they are of the same mind, they are the same thing; and though they are two persons, they are one inasmuch as they have fellowship in the faith, even though they are different as regards their respective persons.

(10) When, finally, Jewish perversity was so moved at these words of our Lord[3] and vehemently inflamed with anger that the people boldly rushed to take up stones, shouting: "Not for a good work do we stone You, but for blasphemy, and because You, being a man, make Yourself God,"[4] the Lord made a distinction when He explained to them precisely in what manner He had said or wished it to be understood that He was God. He said: "Do you say of Him whom the Father has made holy and sent into this world, 'You blaspheme,' because I said, 'I am the Son of God'?"[5] (11) Here again He said that He had a Father. He is therefore the Son, not the Father; for He would have acknowledged Himself to be the Father had He had it in mind that He was the Father. (12) Furthermore, He declares that He has been made holy by His Father. Since, then, He receives sanctification from the Father, He is less than the Father. Because He is less than the Father, He is consequently <not the Father>, but the Son. For if He had been the Father, He would have given, not received sanctification. By openly acknowledging that He receives sanctification from the Father, He proves, by the very fact that He receives sanctification from the Father, that He is less than the Father; consequently He has already demonstrated that He is the Son, not the Father. (13) Furthermore, He says that He has been sent, so that the Lord Christ, coming as He did through obedience, might prove,

3 Viz. "I and the Father are one" (John 10.30).
4 John 10.33.
5 John 10.36.

having been sent, that He was not the Father but the Son, who
certainly would have been the sender if He had been the Father. The
Father, however, was not sent, lest the Father, by being sent, would
prove to be subject to another god. (14) After all that has been said
and done, He still adds what should completely settle every doubt
and put an end to the whole misleading controversy. He says, in fact,
toward the latter part of His discourse: "Do you say, 'You blaspheme' because I said, 'I am the Son of God'?"[6] If, therefore, the
Lord clearly testifies that He is the Son, not the Father, it is a sign of
great rashness and much madness to engage in controversy over the
divinity and over religion, contrary to the testimony of the Lord
Christ Himself, and to say that Christ Jesus is the Father, when one
observes that He has already proved that He is not the Father, but
the Son.

Chapter 28

I will also add that famous passage the heretic holds as dear as the
apple of his own eye, even though he has lost the eye of truth and
light; and in so doing I will force him to acknowledge the complete
blindness of his error. (2) Again and again they bring before me the
very same objection, namely, that it is written: "Have I been so long
a time with you, and you do not know Me? Philip, he who sees Me
sees also the Father."[1] (3) Now let the heretic learn what he does
not understand. Philip is blamed, and rightly and deservedly so,
because he had said: "Lord, show us the Father and it is enough for
us."[2] For when had he ever heard from Christ or been taught that
Christ was the Father? On the contrary, he had frequently heard
and had often been taught that He was the Son, not that He was the
Father, (4) When the Lord said: "If you have known Me, you have
also known My Father; and henceforth you know Him, and you
have seen Him,"[3] He did not say it in such a manner as to wish

6 *Ibid.*

1 John 14.9.
2 John 14.8.
3 John 14.7.

Himself to be taken for the Father. Rather, it means that the man
who completely and perfectly, with full faith and devotion, has
drawn near the Son of God shall certainly through the Son in whom
he so believes, attain to the Father and shall see Him. (5) "For no
one," He says, "can come to the Father but through Me."[4] Therefore not only shall he come to God the Father and know the Father
Himself but he also ought to keep himself in such a state of mind
and anticipation as though he already knew the Father and saw Him
as well.

(6) For Divine Scripture often mentions things that have not yet
been done as already done, because they are eventually going to be
done; and it foretells things which are certainly about to happen, not
as though they are going to happen in the future, but rather as
though they had already happened.[5] (7) In fact, though Christ had
not yet been born in the time of Isaiah the prophet, Isaiah stated:
"For a child is born to us."[6] And although Mary had not yet been
approached, he said: "And I went to the prophetess and she conceived and bore a son."[7] (8) Though Christ had not yet made known
the divine secrets of the Father, Isaiah stated: "And His name will be
called the Angel of Great Counsel."[8] (9) He had not yet suffered,
and the prophet declared: "He was led as a sheep to the
throat-cutter."[9] (10) As yet there had been no Cross, and he stated:
"All the day long have I stretched out My hands to an unbelieving
people."[10] (11) He had not as yet, in scorn, been proffered drink,
and the prophet says: "In My thirst they gave Me vinegar to
drink."[11] (12) Though He had not yet been divested, he declared:
"Upon My vesture they cast lots; and they numbered My bones;
they pierced My hands and feet."[12] (13) For divine Scripture, which

4 John 14.6.
5 The prophet, seeing future events vividly portrayed in his prophetic vision,
  describes them as though they were present or already past; hence, he
  makes use of the present and the past, instead of the future.
6 Isa. 9.6.
7 Isa. 8.3; Novatian's text shows the third person ("he went").
8 Isa. 9.6.
9 Isa. 53.7.
10 Isa. 65.2.
11 Ps. 68(69).22.
12 Ps 21(22),19, 18, 17.

foresees all, speaks of things which it knows will take place in the future, as already done. And it speaks of things as already accomplished which it regards as future, because they undoubtedly shall come to pass. (14) In the present passage, therefore, the Lord stated: "Henceforth you do know Him and you have seen Him."[13] He said that whoever followed the Son would see the Father. He did not mean that the Son Himself was the Father, now seen, but that whoever was willing to follow Him and become His disciple would obtain the reward of being able to see the Father. (15) He is also the image of God the Father; therefore this truth can be added to the others: As the Father works, so does the Son also; and the Son is the imitator of all His Father's works.[14] Accordingly, every man can feel that, in a sense, he has already seen the Father, inasmuch as he sees Him who always imitates the invisible Father in all His works.

(16) Furthermore, if Christ is the Father Himself, how is it that He immediately goes on to say: "He who believes in Me, the works that I do he shall do, and greater than these he shall do because I am going to the Father"? [15] (17) And then He adds: "If you love Me, keep My commandments. And I will ask the Father and He will give you another Advocate."[16] (18) After saying all these things, He even adds that well-known passage: "If anyone love Me, he will keep My word, and my Father loves him, and We will come to him and make Our abode with him."[17] (19) Nor did He omit that other passage: "But the Advocate, the Holy Spirit, whom the Father will send, He will teach you and bring to your mind whatever I have said to you."[18] (20) He places before us still another passage to prove that He is the Son and therefore says: "If you loved Me, you would rejoice that I am going to the Father, for the Father is greater than I." [19] (21) What will the heretic reply when He also adds that passage: "I am the true vine, and My Father is the vine-dresser. Every

13 John 14.7.
14 Cf. John 5.19, 17.
15 John 14.12.
16 John 14.15-16.
17 John 14.23.
18 John 14.26.
19 John 14.28.

branch in Me that bears no fruit He takes away; and every branch that bears fruit He cleanses, that it may bear more fruit"? [20] (22) Still He presses on and adds: "As the Father has loved Me, I also have loved you. Abide in My love. If you keep My commandments, you will abide in My love, as I also have kept My Father's commandments, and abide in His love."[21] (23) He yet heaps sentence upon sentence and says: "But I have called you friends, because all things that I have heard from My Father, I have made known to you."[22] (24) And on the top of the heap He even adds: "But all these things they will do to you for My name's sake, because they do not know Him who sent Me."[23]

(25) The Lord, therefore, would never have used all these arguments, especially after having already given so many that clearly bear witness that He is not the Father but the Son, if He had been mindful that He was the Father or wished that He be considered the Father. His sole purpose in these words was to make it clear to us that every man should henceforth account it to be the same thing to see the image of God the Father through the Son, as if he had seen the Father. Every man, by believing in the Son, exercises himself in the contemplation of the Image, that he may advance and grow even to the perfect contemplation of God the almighty Father, after he has grown accustomed to see the divinity in the Image. Furthermore, he who has imbued his mind and spirit with this truth and has believed that it will be so without exception has already, in a sense, seen the Father, whom he shall see hereafter. Already has he here on earth, as though it were in his grasp, what he knows for certain he will one day have.

(26) Furthermore, if Christ had been the Father Himself, why did He promise, as though it were a future reward, what He had already bestowed and granted? (27) When He says: "Blessed are the clean of heart, for they shall see God,"[24] we find Him promising the contem-

---

20 John 15.1-2.
21 John 15.9-10.
22 John 15.15.
23 John 15.21.
24 Matt. 5.8.

plation and vision of the Father. Therefore, He had not yet granted it; for why would He promise it, if He had already granted it? He would have given it, were He the Father; for He was being seen and had been touched. (28) When Christ Himself is seen and touched by the crowd and yet promises and declares that he who is clean of heart shall see God, He proves by this very fact that He, who was then present, was not the Father because He promised, while actually present to their gaze, that whoever was clean of heart would see the Father. (29) He, therefore, who was promising these things, was not the Father, but the Son; for He who was the Son promised what would be seen hereafter. His promise would have been meaningless, had He not been the Son. Why did He promise the clean of heart that they would see the Father, if those who were then present were already seeing Christ, the Father? However, because He was the Son and not the Father, it was fitting that the Son, inasmuch as He is the Image of the Father, should be then seen; and the Father, because He is invisible, is deservedly promised and designated as the one who would be seen by the clean of heart.

(30) Let these few words, therefore, which I have expressed about so many questions, suffice against that heretic. For a broad and spacious field will open before us, if we would wish to further pursue this particular heretic. Now that he has been deprived of those two passages, he is like a man who has had his two eyes gouged out;[25] he is completely overcome by the blindness of his own doctrine.

Chapter 29

Next, well-ordered reason and the authority of our faith bid us (in the words and the writings of our Lord set down in orderly fashion) to believe, after these things, also in the Holy Spirit, who was in times past promised to the Church and duly bestowed at the appointed, favorable moment. (2) He was indeed promised by the

---

25 Novatian now claims that he has deprived his "heretical Cyclops" of all vision, leaving him utterly vanquished in the blindness of his error. Cf. *supra* 28.1.

prophet Joel but bestowed through Christ. "In the last days," says the prophet, "I will pour out from My spirit upon My servants and handmaids."[1] And the Lord said: "Receive the Holy Spirit; whose sins you shall forgive, they are forgiven; and whose sins you shall retain, they are retained."[2] (3) Now the Lord sometimes calls the Holy Spirit the Paraclete and at other times proclaims Him to be the Spirit of truth.[3] He is not new in the Gospel, nor has He been given in a novel way. For it was He who in the prophets reproved the people and in the apostles gave an invitation to the Gentiles.[4] The former deserved to be reproved because they disregarded the Law, and those of the Gentiles who believe deserve to be assisted by the patronage of the Spirit, because they ardently desire to attain to the Law of the Gospel. (4) There are, undoubtedly, different kinds of functions in Him, since different times have different kinds of needs; yet He who acts thus is not different on that account. Nor is He someone else because He acts so; rather He is the selfsame one, distributing His functions according to the times, conditions, and circumstances of human events.[5] (5) Accordingly the apostle Paul says: "Since we have the same spirit, as shown in that which is written: 'I believed, and so I spoke,' we also believe and so we speak."[6] (6) Therefore, it is one and the same Spirit who is in the prophets and in the apostles. He was, however, in the former only for awhile; whereas He abides in the latter forever. In other words, He is in the prophets but not to remain always in them, in the apostles, that He might abide in them forever. He has been apportioned to the former in moderation; to the latter, He has been wholly poured out, He was sparingly given to the one; upon the other, lavishly bestowed.[7] He was not, however, manifested before the

1 Joel 3.2 (Vulgate 2.29).
2 John 20.22-23.
3 Cf. John 14.16-17; 15.26.
4 Cf. Gregory of Elvira, *Tract. Orig.* 20, lines 54-61 (CCL 69.143). Against the Marcionites, Novatian upholds the unity of the Holy Spirit's action under the two dispensations. In the Old Testament, He had threatened to forsake the Jews; in the New Testament, He fulfilled the threat.
5 Cf. Rom. 12.6; 1 Cor. 12.4.
6 2 Cor. 4.13.
7 Cf. John 3.34.

Lord's Resurrection but conferred by Christ's Resurrection. (7) In fact, Christ said: "I will ask the Father, and He will give you another Advocate that He may be with you forever, the Spirit of truth",[8] and "When the Advocate has come whom I will send you from My Father, the Spirit of truth, who proceeds from My Father";[9] and "If I do not go, the Advocate will not come to you; but if I go, I will send Him to you";[10] and "when the Spirit of truth has come, He will guide you to all truth."[11] (8) Since the Lord was about to go to heaven, He had to give the Paraclete to His disciples, that He might not leave them as orphans,[12] as it were, and abandon them without a defender or some sort of guardian. That would not have been proper at all.

(9) It is He who strengthened their hearts and minds, who clearly brought out for them the mysteries of the Gospel, who was within them the enlightener of divine things; through strength given by Him they feared neither bonds nor imprisonment for the sake of the Lord's name. Yes, they even trampled underfoot the very powers and torments of the world, because they were already armed and fortified through Him and possessed within themselves the gifts which this same Spirit distributes and consigns,[13] as if they were ornaments, to the Church, the Bride of Christ.[14] (10) In fact, it is He who places prophets in the Church, instructs teachers, bestows the gift of tongues, effects cures and miracles, does wondrous deeds, grants the power of discerning spirits, confers the power of administration, suggests[15] what decisions should be made, and sets in order and arranges whatever charismatic gifts there are. Thus, He makes the Church of the Lord perfect and complete in every respect and in every detail.

(11) He it is who came upon the Lord as a dove after He had been

8 John 14.16-17.
9 John 15.26.
10 John 16.7.
11 John 16.13.
12 Cf. John 14.18.
13 Cf. 1 Cor. 12.8-11, 28.
14 Cf. Gregory of Elvira, *Tract. Orig.* 20, lines 150-59 (CCL 69.146).
15 The assistance of the Holy Spirit is described in the documents of the Church as a *suggestio* and *edoctio.*

baptized, and abode in Him.[16] In Christ alone He dwells fully and entirely, not wanting in any measure[17] or part; but in all His overflowing abundance dispensed and sent forth, so that other men might receive from Christ a first outpouring, as it were, of His graces. For the fountainhead of the entire Holy Spirit abides in Christ, that from Him might be drawn streams of grace and wondrous deeds because the Holy Spirit dwells affluently in Christ. (12) In fact, Isaiah prophesied this when he said: "And the spirit of wisdom and of understanding rests upon Him, the spirit of counsel and might, the spirit of knowledge and piety, and the spirit of the fear of the Lord shall fill Him."[18] (13) He reiterated the very same thing in another passage in the person of the Lord Himself: "The Spirit of the Lord is upon Me, because He has anointed Me; to bring good news to the poor He has sent Me."[19] (14) Likewise David says: "Therefore God, your God, has anointed you with the oil of gladness above your fellow kings."[20] (15) The apostle Paul says of Him: "For he who does not have the Spirit of Christ, he does not belong to Christ";[21] and, "where the Spirit of the Lord is, there is freedom."[22]

(16) He it is who effects from water a second birth,[23] the seed, as it were, of a divine generation. He is also the consecrator of a heavenly birth,[24] "the pledge" of a promised "inheritance,"[25] a kind of written bond, so to speak, of eternal salvation. He it is who makes us

---

16 Cf. Matt. 3.16; Mark 1.10; Luke 3.22; John 1.33.
17 Cf. John 3.34.
18 Isa 11.2. We find the number seven already in St. Justin, *Dialogus cum Tryphone* 87.
19 Isa. 61.1.
20 Ps. 44(45).8.
21 Rom. 8.9.
22 2 Cor. 3.17.
23 A reference to the sacrament of baptism; cf. ch. 10.9. Subsequently Novatian's followers, willing to deny the validity of baptism already administered in the Church, were accustomed to rebaptize those who passed over from the Church to their schismatic movement (cf. Cyprian, *Ep.* 73: CSEL 3.2.779.10).
24 This is possibly a reference to the sacrament of confirmation.
25 Eph. 1.14.

the temple of God[26] and makes us His dwelling place. He importunes the divine ears "on our behalf with ineffable groanings,"[27] thereby discharging His duties as Advocate and rendering His services in our defense. He has been given to dwell in our bodies and to bring about our sanctification. He brings our bodies, by this operation of His in us, to eternity and to the resurrection of immortality,[28] inasmuch as He accustoms them to be mingled in Himself with celestial power and to be associated with the divine eternity of His Holy Spirit. (17) For in Him and through Him, our bodies are trained to advance to immortality, learning to bridle themselves with moderation according to His commands. (18) For it is He who lusts against the flesh, because the flesh is contrary to Him.[29] (19) It is He who checks insatiable desires, breaks unbridled lust, quenches illicit passions, overcomes fiery assaults, averts drunkenness, resists avarice, drives away wanton revelries, binds together noble loves, strengthens good affections, does away with factions, explains the Rule of Truth, refutes heretics, banishes the impious and guards the Gospels.[30]

(20) Of Him the Apostle likewise writes: "Now we have received not the spirit of the world, but the Spirit that is from God."[31] (21) Of Him he exults when he says: "But I think that I also have the Spirit of God."[32] (22) Of Him he says: "And the spirit of the prophets is under the control of the prophets."[33] (23) Of Him he states: "Now the Spirit expressly says that in after times some will depart from the faith, giving heed to deceitful spirits and doctrines of devils, speaking lies hypocritically, and having their conscience

26 Cf. 1 Cor. 3.16-17; 2 Cor. 6.16.
27 Rom. 8.26.
28 In the exercise of virtue, man is under the action of the Holy Spirit who dwells in him, effects his sanctification, and brings his body to a glorious resurrection. Elsewhere Novatian states that the aid which prods man to do good is a "gift of God" (cf. *De bon. pud.* 4.3, 14.3: CCL 4.116, 127).
29 Cf. Gal. 5.17.
30 A beautiful third-century affirmation that the Holy Spirit is keeper of Holy Writ.
31 1 Cor. 2.12.
32 1 Cor. 7.40.
33 1 Cor. 14.32.

seared."[34] (24) Grounded in this Spirit, "no one" ever "says 'Anathema' to Jesus";[35] no one has denied that Christ is the Son of God, nor has rejected God the Creator; no one utters any words against the Scriptures: no one lays down alien and sacrilegious ordinances; no one makes contradictory laws. (25) Whoever "shall have blasphemed" against Him, "does not have forgiveness, either in this world or in the world to come."[36] (26) It is He who in the apostles renders testimony to Christ, in the martyrs manifests the unwavering faith of religion, in virgins encloses the admirable continence of sealed chastity. In the rest of men, He keeps the laws of the Lord's teaching uncorrupted and untainted. He destroys heretics, corrects those in error, reproves unbelievers, reveals impostors, and also corrects the wicked. He keeps the Church uncorrupted and inviolate in the holiness of perpetual virginity and truth.[37]

Chapter 30

What we have stated briefly, discussed concisely, and presented succinctly concerning the Father, Son, and Holy Spirit—let these things now suffice. They could indeed have been propounded at greater length and drawn out with more solid argumentation, because the entire Old and New Testaments could have been brought forth to prove that such is the true faith. (2) The heretics, however, in their persistent opposition to the truth, are wont to draw out their controversy with the Catholic faith and genuine tradition. They are scandalized by Christ because the Scriptures assert that He is also God and we believe this. Therefore, that all heretical calumny against our Faith may cease, it is right that we should discuss the fact that Christ is also God (in such a way that it will not interfere with the truth of Scripture or with our faith) because the Scriptures assert and because we maintain and believe that there is only one God.

34 1 Tim. 4.1-2.
35 1 Cor. 12.3.
36 Matt. 12.32; Mark 3.29; Luke 12.10.
37 Cf. 2 Cor. 11.2; Gregory of Elvira, *Tract. Orig.* 20, lines 93-145, 133 (CCL 69.144-45)

(3) In fact, the heretics who say that Jesus Christ is Himself God the Father, as well as those who would have had Him to be only a man, have drawn from Scripture the elements and the reasons for their error and perversity. For when they observed that it was written that God is one, they thought that they could not hold such a belief unless they thought they should believe that Christ was a mere man or that He was really God the Father. Wherefore they were accustomed to put their calumnies in syllogistic form to try to justify their own error. (4) Now, the heretics[1] who say that Jesus Christ is the Father argue as follows: If God is one and Christ is God, then Christ is the Father, because God is one. If Christ is not the Father, while Christ, the Son, is also God, then two gods seem to have been introduced, contrary to the Scriptures. (5) On the other hand, the heretics[2] who maintain that Christ is only a man syllogize from the opposite position in the following manner: If the Father is one and the Son another and if the Father is God and Christ is God, then there is not one God, but there are two gods introduced on an equal footing: the Father and the Son. If there is one God, then Christ must be a man so that the Father may rightly be the one God. (6) Indeed, the Lord is crucified, as it were, between two thieves, just as He was once crucified;[3] thus He is exposed on either side to the impious revilings of these heretics.

(7) However, neither do the Holy Scriptures nor do we afford them any ground for their present ruin and blindness, because they either will not, or cannot, see what has been so clearly laid down on the open page of the Divine Writings. (8) Not only do we know but we also read, believe, and maintain that there is one God who made both the heavens and the earth, because we do not know of any other god, nor will we ever be able to learn of another, inasmuch as there is no other. (9) "I am," He says, "God; and there is no other besides Me: a just God and a savior."[4] (10) And in another place, He asserts: "I am the First and the Last, and besides Me there is no God.

1 The Patripassians.
2 The Adoptianists.
3 Cf. Matt. 27.38; Mark 15.27; Luke 23.33; John 19.18.
4 Isa. 43.11; Hosea 13.4.

Who is as I am?"[5] (11) Again He says: "Who has measured the heavens with a span and the earth with the width of the fist? Who has weighed the mountains on scales, and the woods on a balance?"[6] (12) And Hezekiah says: "That all men may know that You alone are God."[7] (13) Furthermore, the Lord Himself says: "Why do you ask Me about what is good? The one God is good."[8] (14) And also Paul the apostle says: "Who alone has immortality and dwells in light inaccessible, whom no man has seen or can see."[9] (15) In another place he also says: "There is no intermediary where there is only one; but God is one."[10] (16) Now just as we hold and read and believe this, so too we must not disregard any part of the Heavenly Scriptures. We must not in any way reject the marks of Christ's divinity which are set down in the Scriptures, that we may not be accused of having violated the integrity of our holy Faith by violating the authority of the Scriptures. (17) And let us, therefore, believe this, since it is a very true saying that Jesus Christ, our Lord and God, is the Son of God: "In the beginning was the Word, and the Word was with God, and the Word was God. He was in the beginning with God. And the Word was made flesh and dwelt among us."[11] (18) It is also written: "My Lord and my God."[12] Finally, it is written: "Of whom are the fathers, and from whom is the Christ according to the flesh, who is, over all things, God blessed forever."[13]

(19) What shall we say, then? Is Scripture placing before us two gods? If so, how does it assert that "there is one God"? [14] Or is it possible that Christ is not also God? If so, what is the meaning of those words addressed to Christ: "My Lord and My God"? [15] (20) Therefore, unless we hold all this with due reverence and sound

5 Isa. 44.6-7.
6 Isa. 40.12.
7 Isa. 37.20; 4 Kings 19.19.
8 Matt. 19.17; Mark 10.18; Luke 18.19.
9 1 Tim. 6.16.
10 Gal. 3.20.
11 John 1.1, 2, 14.
12 John 20.28.
13 Rom. 9.5.
14 Gal. 3.20.
15 John 20.28.

reasoning, we shall assuredly be looked upon as persons who have given the heretics an occasion to err. Certainly, this is not due to any fault of the Heavenly Scriptures, which never can deceive, but rather results from the prejudice of human error, whereby they willed to be heretics. (21) First of all, then, we must refute the argument of those who presume to make against us the charge of saying that there are two gods. (22) It is written, and they cannot deny it, that "there is one Lord."[16] Now, what do they think of Christ? Do they think that He is the Lord or that He is simply not the Lord? On the contrary, there is not the least doubt in their minds that He is the Lord. Therefore, if their reasoning is correct, we have, as a result, two Lords. How is it then that according to the Scriptures there is one Lord? (23) Furthermore, Christ is called "the one Master";[17] yet we read that the apostle Paul is also a master.[18] We no longer have, therefore, one master; for according to these observations, we gather that there are two masters. How, then, is Christ the one Master, according to the Scriptures? (24) In the Scriptures, one is said to be good, God:[19] yet it is likewise said in the Scriptures that Christ is good.[20] They should rightly infer from this, therefore, that there is not one, but two who are good. How, then, is it stated according to the good faith of the Scriptures, that there is one who is good? (25) They do not think that the truth, that there is one Lord, is prejudiced in any way but that other truth, that Christ is also Lord. Nor do we think that the truth, that there is one Master, is prejudiced in any way by the truth, that Paul is also a master. Finally, neither do they assert that the truth, that there is one who is good, is prejudiced in any way by the truth, that Christ is also called good. Let them acknowledge, then, by the same line of reasoning that the truth, that there is one God, is not prejudiced in any way by the other truth, that Christ also is declared to be God.

---

16 Deut. 6.4; Eph. 4.5.
17 Matt. 23.8, 10.
18 Cf. 2 Tim. 1.11.
19 Cf. Matt. 19.17; Mark 10.18; Luke 18.19.
20 Cf. Matt. 19.16; Mark 10.17; Luke 18.18; John 10.11.

Chapter 31

There is, then, God the Father, the Founder and Creator of all things, who alone is without origin, invisible, immense, immortal, eternal, the one God. Nothing whatever, I will not say can be preferred, but can even be compared to His greatness, His majesty, and His power. (2) Of Him when He willed,[1] the Word, who is the Son, was born. The Word is to be understood here not as a sound that strikes the air nor the tone of the voice forced from the lungs,[2] but rather is discerned in the substance of a power proceeding from God. Apostle has never ascertained, prophet has not discovered, angel has not fathomed, nor has any creature known the hallowed secrets of His sacred and divine birth. They are known to the Son alone, who has known the secrets of the Father.[3]

(3) Since He is begotten of the Father, He is always in the Father. I say "always," however, not in such a manner as to prove that He is unborn, but to prove that He is born. Now, He who is before all time must be said to have been always in the Father; for no time can be attributed to Him who is before time. He is always in the Father, lest the Father be not always the Father. On the other hand, the Father also precedes Him; for, as the Father, He must of necessity be prior, because He who knows no origin must of necessity precede Him who has an origin. At the same time the Son must be less than the Father, for He knows that He is in the Father, having an origin, since he is born. Although He has an origin inasmuch as He is born, yet through His Father He is, in a certain manner, like[4] Him by birth, because He

1 Cf. Hippolytus, *Contra haer. Noeti* 10, 11.
2 Novatian's argument is directed against the Modalists. Cf. Tertullian, *Adv. Prax.* 7; Hippolytus, *Philosophumena* 10.33. Modalism defends monotheism rigidly up to the point of conceiving the Trinity of the divine Persons as three modes of being and of self-manifestation of the one God. The same divine Person, insofar as it creates and generates, is Father; insofar as it is generated and redeems men, is Son; insofar as it sanctifies, is Holy Spirit. Modalism does not admit of a real distinction between the three divine Persons.
3 Cf. Matt. 11.27.
4 Cf. Gregory of Nazianzus, *Oratio theologica* 3 (*Orat.* 29) 11 (PG 36.88; tr. by C. G. Browne and J. E. Swallow, in *Nicene and Post-Nicene Fathers* 7 [New York 1894] 304-5); Aeby, *op. cit.* 111.

is born of that Father, who alone has no origin. (4) He, therefore, when the Father willed, proceeded from the Father; and He who was in the Father, because He was of the Father, was afterwards[5] with the Father since He—namely that divine substance whose name is the Word, through whom "all things were made and without whom nothing was made"[6]—proceeded from the Father. (5) For all things are after Him, because they are "through Him";[7] consequently He is before all things (but after the Father), since all things were made through Him. He proceeded from the Father, according to whose will all things were made. God assuredly proceeded from God, constituting as Son the Second Person after the Father, but not taking from the Father that which makes Him one God.[8]

(6) If He had not been born, as unborn He would have been compared with the Father who is unborn. Since an equality would have appeared in both, He would have constituted a second unborn, and therefore two gods. (7) If He had not been begotten, He would have been placed side by side with Him who is not begotten. Since both would have been found to be equal, as unbegotten, they would accordingly have given us two gods; Christ, then, would have given rise to two gods. (8) If He were, as the Father, without an origin, He Himself would also have proved to be, as the Father, the beginning of all things, making two beginnings; consequently He would have also placed before us two gods. (9) Again if He Himself were not the Son, but a Father begetting another son from Himself, then He would have been rightly compared with the Father and would have been shown to be as great as the latter. Thus, He would have constituted two Fathers and approved also of two gods. (10) If He had been invisible, He would have been compared with Him who is invisible and declared equal to Him. He would have placed before us two invisibles; consequently He would have also permitted two gods. (11) If He had been incomprehensible, if He had also possessed whatever other attributes belong to the Father, then we assert that

5 That is, after the *nativitas*; cf. ch. 17.3.
6 John 1.3.
7 *Ibid.*
8 Cf. Arnobius the Younger, *Arnobii Catholici et Serapionis Conflictus de Deo trino et uno* (PL 53.257B/C).

He would have certainly occasioned the controversy of two gods that these heretics raise. (12) As a matter of fact, whatever He is, He is not of Himself because He is not unborn, but is of the Father because He is begotten. For whether He is the Word, whether He is Power, whether He is Wisdom, whether He is Light, whether He is the Son—(13) whatever He is of these, He is not from any other source, but from the Father, as we have already mentioned above. Owing His origin to the Father, He could not cause any disunion in the godhead by making two gods, inasmuch as He drew His origin, in being born, of Him who is the one God. (14) In this respect, since He is the Only-begotten and the First-born of Him who—because He has no origin—is alone the beginning and head of all things, He declared accordingly that God is one. And He proved that He is not subject to any origin or beginning, but rather that He is the origin and the beginning of all things.

(15) The Son does nothing of His own will or counsel and He does not come from Himself. He obeys all His Father's commands and precepts; hence although his birth proves that He is the Son, His docile obedience proclaims Him to be the minister of the will of the Father from whom He is. While He renders Himself obedient to the Father in all things, even though He is also God, yet by His obedience He shows that the Father, from whom He also drew His origin, is the one God.

(16) As a result, He could never constitute a second God because He did not constitute a second origin, inasmuch as He received, before all time, the source of His birth from Him who has no beginning. Since what is unborn and (such is God the Father alone, who is beyond an origin, and from whom is He who is born) is the origin of all other things, He who is born of Him rightly comes from Him who has no origin. This proves that [the Unborn] is the origin from which He Himself is; and even though He who is born is God, nevertheless He shows that God is one whom He who was born has confirmed to be without origin.

(17) Therefore He is God, but begotten precisely that He might be

God. He is also Lord, but for this very reason was He born of the
Father, that He might be Lord. He is also an angel, but an angel who
has been destined by His Father to announce the great counsel of
God.[9] (18) His divinity is so presented to us that it may not appear,
either through discordancy or through inequality in the Godhead,
that there he has produced two Gods. For all things have been
subjected to Him, as Son, by the Father. The fact that He Himself,
together with all the things that are subject to Him, is subject to His
Father[10] proves that He is indeed the Son of His Father; however,
He is considered the Lord and God of all else. (19) Because all
subjected things are given over to Him who is God, and the Son is
indebted to the Father for the subjection of all things to Himself, He
refers back again to the Father the entire power of the Godhead.
(20) Hence one God is demonstrated, the true and eternal Father,
from whom alone this power of the Godhead is sent forth, trans-
mitted, and directed to the Son, and is returned again, by communion of substance, to the Father. (21) The Son is indeed shown
to be God, since it is clear that the divinity has been handed over
and granted to Him. Nevertheless, the Father proves to be one God;
for from one order to another that divine Majesty makes its way
back again to the Father and reverts to Him who gave it, since the
Son Himself delivers it up again to Him. (22) Thus "the Mediator
between God and men, Christ Jesus"[11] has power—since He is God—
over every creature subjected to Him by His own Father, together
with all creation subject to Him. Found also to be in harmony with
God, His Father, Christ Jesus, by abiding in Him (because He also
was heard),[12] has succinctly proved that His Father is the one and
only true God.

9 Cf. Isa. 9.6.
10 Cf. 1 Cor. 15.25-28.
11 1 Tim. 2.5.
12 The last passage of the text is so hopelessly corrupt that there must be
   doubt as to what Scripture, if any, Novatian had in mind. "Because He also
   was heard" may be a reference to Heb. 5.7; "abiding in Him," to John
   14.10.

THE SPECTACLES

INTRODUCTION

S HAS BEEN STATED in the General Introduction Novatian's *Spectacles*, as well as *In Praise of Purity*, survived under the name of St. Cyprian. A study of its style and content led towards the end of the nineteenth century to its definitive attribution to Novatian. This work and Novatian's *Jewish Foods* and *In Praise of Purity* form a trilogy of pastoral letters. In all three the author, absent from his community, admonishes his adherents to remain steadfast in the Gospel. He finds no better way to accomplish this than to treat one topic or another in Christian morality.[1]

The Spectacles begins, as does also *Jewish Foods,* with the inscription, "Novatian to the people who stand firm in the Gospel." It is divided into two parts (chs. 2-8; 9-10), with an introduction (ch. 1) and a conclusion (ch. 10).

Novatian complains that he is greatly troubled that he cannot always write to his flock. He has no misgivings about their conduct; they remain faithful to their profession of faith. Unfortunately, however, advocates of vice and error are never wanting. These champions of vice have the audacity to use the authority of Holy Scripture to condone attendance at the spectacles (ch. 1), the races, the fights in the amphitheater, the theater, and the like.

In chapter 2 and subsequent chapters, Novatian manifests a predilection for the phrase *Christianus fidelis* ("faithful Christian").[2] The term *Christianus* includes the catechumens, that is, the aspirants to baptism who were being carefully prepared for Christian initiation. The organization of the catechumenate varied from church to

1 D'Alès, *op. cit.* 157-158.
2 H. Koch, "Codex Parisinus 1658 e lo scritto pseudociprianeo (novazianeo) De spectaculis," *Religio* 12 (1936) 246; *Spect.*, chs. 2.1-3; 3.2; 4.2, 4; 6.3; 7.1, 3; 8.2; 9.3; 10.1.

church, but generally included two classes of candidates: *audientes* (auditors) and *competentes* (catechumens), corresponding to the two periods of preparation: remote, which lasted up to three years, and proximate, which coincided wholly or partially with Lent and closed with the conferring of baptism on the night before Easter Sunday, when the *competentes* became *faithful* or *neophytes* (regenerated).[3] The term *fidelis*, therefore, designates only a baptized person. Novatian makes use of the strong phrase *Christianus fidelis* to designate a baptized Christian who has all the obligations of a full-fledged Christian and whose failings are graver than those of an unbaptized Christian.[4]

Novatian is astonished to find faithful Christians attending the spectacles. They are not ashamed to defend by means of Holy Writ the pagan superstitions and the idolatry that are inherent in such spectacles (ch. 2). The texts which they cite, replies Novatian, are merely exhortations to practice evangelical virtue, not concessions to attend pagan spectacles and enjoy base pleasures (ch. 3). Even the devil can cite Scripture for his purpose.

Sacred Scripture condemns the spectacles because idolatry is the source of all the public games. How incongruous it is for a faithful Christian, who has renounced the devil at baptism, to renounce Christ at the games! Romulus was the first to consecrate the circus games to Consus—the God of Counsel; later, amusements were dedicated to Ceres and Bacchus (ch. 4).

At times, human sacrifices take place at the games, as a pledge to a thirsting idol. Who can assess the moral damage? Bloody spectacles teach brutality. Wild beasts are carefully trained to inflict pain on human beings and to perform with greater fury. The spectacles foment quarrels, vanity, and discord. So much bickering over the different chariots, over mere questions of vainglory; rejoicing that one horse was faster than another! And Novatian satirically continues: there are those who can tell a horse's pedigree for generations

---

3 A. Stenzel, "Temporal and Supra-Temporal in the History of the Catechumenate and Baptism," *Concilium* 22 (1967) 31-44.
4 Koch, *op. cit.* 247; Diercks, *op. cit.* 154-56.

but are ignorant of the Gospel story.[5] Finally, the spectacles teach immorality. If you ask the spectators what road they took to get to the games, they will admit: "by way of a brothel, the naked bodies of prostitutes, wanton licentiousness, public vice, and notorious lechery" (ch. 5.4).

What is more, they even take the Holy Eucharist with them into such places. A spectator rushes over to the public display after dismissal from the Lord's sacrifice, still bearing with him, as is the custom, the Eucharist; that faithless man has carried into the midst of the foul bodies of prostitutes the sacred Body of the Lord (ch. 5.5). After fifteen centuries we find Novatian's strictures confirmed from the Holy See. Pope Paul VI, in his Encyclical Letter on the Holy Eucharist of September 3, 1965, entitled *Mysterium Fidei*, attests to the latreutic worship the Church has always offered and still offers to the Sacrament of the Eucharist, both during Mass and outside it. He writes:

> In the oldest documents of the Church we have many testimonies of this veneration. The shepherds of the Church in fact, solicitously exhorted the faithful to take the greatest care in keeping the Eucharist which they took to their homes. . . . *Novatian, who is a reliable witness in this matter*, states that these same shepherds severely censured any lack of due reverence that may have crept in. He considers that person "who after dismissal from the Lord's sacrifice and still bearing with him, as is the custom, the Eucharist, the sacred Body of the Lord, and not going to his home, but running off to the theater" as worthy of condemnation.[6]

At the theater, obscenity, public wantonness, and impurity reign supreme. "What is a faithful Christian doing there," asks Novatian, "when he is not even allowed to think of evil?" (ch. 6) The theater surpasses the foulness of the brothel. All

---

5 Fausset, *Novatiani. . .De Trinitate Liber* xx.
6 Pope Paul VI, *Encyclical Letter on the Holy Eucharist: Mysterium Fidei* (Washington, D.C.: National Catholic Welfare Conference 1965) 16-17. The italics are mine.

the spectacles—be they comedies, tragedies, musical concerts or gladiatorial contests—are replete with peril and vanity. Even if such spectacles were not consecrated to idols, they must be abhorred by faithful Christians (chs. 7-8).

In the second part, Novatian exclaims: "A Christian has, if he so wills, better spectacles" (ch. 9.1). He has this beautiful world to admire: sunrise and sunset, the moon's waxings and wanings, the glittering stars moving in harmony, the changes of the seasons, days turning to night and nights to day, the mountains, meandering streams, the great expanses of the sea with its breakers and shore-lines, the fishes, the birds, and man. The playhouses may glisten with gold, but they are no match for the splendor of the stars (*ibid.*).

Sacred Scripture will provide the faithful Christian with spectacles that are in keeping with his faith: the creation of the world and man, the fall of man, the history of the people of God, the resurrection of the dead, the heroism of the martyrs, the devil lying prone under Christ's feet, the work of salvation. Neither praetor nor consul can present such spectacles, only God can do so (ch. 10).

In his *Spectacles* Novatian was inspired by Tertullian, who in A.D. 197 had written a 30-chapter treatise under the same title; he also borrowed from Cyprian's *Ad Donatum.*[7] It is not certain in what period of his life Novatian composed his work. The common opinion, and possibly the true one, is that it was written after Novatian's consecration as bishop.[8]

The present translation is based on the critical texts of W. Hartel, CSEL 3.3 (1871), and A. Boulanger (Paris 1933), but full account has been taken of the edition in CCL 4 (Turnhout 1972).

---

7 Both works have been translated in this series: that of Tertullian (by E. A. Quain), FC 40.30-107; that of Cyprian (by R. J. Deferrari), FC 36.3-21.

8 Diercks, CCL.xii, presents the argument of H. J. Vogt that places the work prior to the Decian persecution.

SELECT BIBLIOGRAPHY

Texts:

Diercks, G. F. *Novatiani opera* . . . (CCL 4) 153-79.
Hartel, W. CSEL 3.3 (1871) 1-13.
Boulanger, A. *Tertullien, De spectaculis, suivi de Pseudo-Cyprien, De spectaculis* (Paris 1933).

Translations:

Wallis, R. E. in *Ante-Nicene Christian Library* 13 (Edinburgh 1880) 221-30; *The Ante-Nicene Fathers* 5 (New York 1899) 575-78.

Secondary Sources:

D'Alès, A. *Novatien: Étude sur la théologie romaine au milieu du IIIe siècle* (Paris 1925).
Koch, H. "Codex Parisinus 1658 e lo scritto pseudociprianeo (novazianeo) De spectaculis," *Religio* 12 (1936) 245-265.
Melin, B. *Studia in Corpus Cyprianeum* (Uppsala 1946).
Quasten, J. *Patrology* 2.223-24.

CONTENTS

THE SPECTACLES

Novatian [sends] his greetings to the people who stand firm in the Gospel.[1]

T GRIEVES ME and sorely troubles my spirit when I have no opportunity of writing to you. It is a loss to me when I cannot speak with you. Likewise, nothing makes me so happy and truly delights me as to have that opportunity once again. I feel that I am present with you when I speak to you by letter. (2) I know that you are convinced that what I tell you is so, and that you do not doubt the truth of my words, but even so, proof attests the sincerity of a matter. I show my devotion to you by not letting slip by a single opportunity of writing to you. (3) I am quite certain that your daily life is laudable and that you remain faithful to your profession of faith. Nonetheless, ingratiating champions and indulgent advocates of vice are never lacking to justify their own vicious practices. What is worse, they transform the censure that the heavenly Scriptures pronounce on such matters into a plea for their own misdeeds. They would have it that the pleasure one gets from the spectacles is blameless because it is merely a means of mental relaxation. The strength of ecclesiastical discipline is greatly weakened and ruined by the enervating influence of vice. In consequence vice is not only exculpated—it actually wins for itself greater authorization. In these few words I have no intention of teaching you anything. You, who have already been instructed, should take care lest wounds whose edges have been

1 Cf. 1 Cor. 15.1.

poorly joined together may break through the cicatrization formed in a superficial healing. (4) We overcome with greatest difficulty an evil that easily returns, especially if it has the approval and blandishing condonation of the crowd.[2]

Chapter 2

Among the faithful and those who lay claim to the dignity of a Christian calling, some find no shame—no shame, I say—in vindicating, from the heavenly Scriptures, the vain superstitions of the pagans that are intermingled in the spectacles and thus conferring divine authority upon idolatry.[1] (2) When the pagans do anything in honor of one of their idols and the spectacle is frequented by faithful Christians, not only is pagan idolatry defended but religion—the true and divine religion—is trampled on in contempt of God. A sense of decency keeps me from relating their evasive defense and their pleas in this matter. (3) "Where," they ask, "are such things mentioned in Scripture? Where are they prohibited? On the contrary, not only was Elijah the charioteer of Israel,[2] but even David danced before the ark.[3] In Scripture, we also read of nablas, kinnors, timbrels, flutes, citharas, and dancing troupes.[4] A struggling apostle paints for us the picture of a boxing match and of our own wrestling against the spiritual forces of wickedness.[5] Furthermore, when he makes use of illustrations taken from the footrace, he also mentions the usual prize—the wreath or garland.[6] Why, then, should a faithful

---

2 Novatian was inspired by Tertullian, who had written a treatise (30 chs.) with the same title about the year A.D. 197; he also borrowed from Cyprian's *Ad Donatum*.

---

1 For the idolatrous character of the spectacles, see Irenaeus, *Adv. haereses* 1.1.12; Tertullian, *De spectaculis* 4-13 (tr. R. Arbesmann, O.S.A., FC 40.56-82).
2 Cf. 4 Kings (2 Kings) 2.12.
3 Cf. 2 Kings (2 Sam.) 6.14.
4 Cf. 2 Kings (2 Sam.) 6.5; 1 Par. (1 Chron.) 15.28-29; Ps 32(33).2; 1 Macc. 13.51.
5 Cf. Eph. 6.12; 1 Cor. 9.26.
6 Cf. 1 Cor. 9.24-25.

Christian not be at liberty to be a spectator of things that the divine Writings are at liberty to mention? " (4) I can, with reason, state here that it would have been far better for such people to lack knowledge of the Scriptures, than to read them in such a manner. Words and noble deeds which have been put down in writing to stimulate us in the practice of evangelical virtue are misinterpreted by them as so many incentives for the practice of vice. These things were written not to make spectators of us, but to incite our minds to greater enthusiasm for salutary things, given that the pagans show great enthusiasm for things far from salutary.

Chapter 3

It is, therefore, a question of instilling virtue—not permission or, if you will, license to become a spectator of pagan aberrations. Just as one endures all manner of hardships and agonizing pain [in the games] to attain to some sort of earthly gain, the thought of attaining eternal rewards should likewise inflame the mind to practice evangelical virtue. (2) That Elijah was the charioteer of Israel is no endorsement of chariot racing; he did not race in the amphitheater. And that David danced before the Lord does in no way encourage faithful Christians to take seats in the theater. He did not distort his body in obscene movements and dance out the drama of Grecian libido. The nablas, kinnors, flutes, timbrels, and citharas played to the Lord—not to an idol.[1] Therefore, no approval whatever is given for spectators of illicit things. (3) Through the devil's artifice, things that were holy are changed into illicit things. If the Holy Scriptures cannot, one's own sense of decency should object to such things. Certain things, you can be sure, are forbidden even more when Scripture does not lay down definite precepts. Out of regard for modesty, Scripture's sheer silence often loudly proclaims what it

---

1 The Boulanger text (p. 101) yields the following translation: "served the Lord, not idols." I follow Koch, *op. cit.* 256-57.—For the instruments see Alfred Sendrey, *Music in Ancient Israel* (New York 1969), esp. ch. 6; E. Gerson-Kiwi, art. "Music, Hebrew," NCE 10.93-94.

roundly condemns. It fears that it would have little regard for its faithful followers if it descended so low. Generally, when it comes to injunctions, it is far better silently to pass over such matters. (4) What is forbidden often incites us. Although certain matters—not recorded in the divine Writings—are passed over in silence, gravity speaks in place of injunctions and right reason admonishes where Scripture is silent. (5) If any man takes careful thought within himself and converses with the inward voice of his [Christian] profession,[2] he will never do anything improper. The conscience that relies solely on itself has the greater weight.

Chapter 4

What has Scripture condemned? It has forbidden us to be spectators of whatever it has forbidden us to do. It condemned, I maintain, all spectacles of this sort when it did away with idolatry—the mother of all the games—from which these monstrosities of vanity and levity take their origin. (2) What spectacle is there without an idol? Is there a game without some sort of sacrifice? Is there a contest that is not dedicated to some dead person? If a faithful Christian really abhors idolatry, then what is he doing among such things? Why does he who is now holy take delight in things that are sinful? Why does he approve of superstitious practices that go contrary to God? He shows his love for them whenever he becomes a spectator of them. (3) Furthermore, he should realize that all these things are machinations of the devil, not of God. In the assembly of the faithful he brazenly exorcises demons whose enticing pleasures he lauds in the spectacles. And though he renounced the devil once and for all, he brings to naught everything that was wrought in baptism. After [professing] Christ, he attends a spectacular of the devil. In so doing, he renounces Christ just as if he were the devil. (4) Idolatry, as I have already stated, is the mother of all the games. To draw faithful Christians, idolatry lures them with extravaganzas to delight their eyes and ears. Romulus was the first to consecrate

---

2 Wallis (ANF 5.576) translates: ". . . speak[s] consistently with the character of his profession."

circus games to Consus—the god of counsel, as it were—in reference to the carrying off of the Sabine women.[1] They that followed him consecrated games to the other gods. When famine held the city in its grip, theatrical amusements were added. These amusements were dedicated to Ceres and Bacchus and, later, to the rest of the idols and to the dead, (5) The celebrated Grecian contests—whether they deal with poetry, or musical instrumentation, or speech, or feats of strength—have diverse demons as their patrons. And anything else that draws the eyes and soothes the ears of the spectators has at bottom either an idol, or a demon, or some deceased person. You have only to look into its origin and foundation. Thus it was all devised by the devil because he knew full well that idolatry of itself is horrendous. He combined idolatry with the spectacles so that idolatry would be loved through the pleasure that the spectacles afforded.

Chapter 5

It is not necessary that I go into further detail and describe for you the monstrous kinds of sacrifices current in the games whereby even a man, at times, becomes a sacrificial victim because of sacerdotal chicanery. Blood from the jugular is still hot when it is received into the spuming libation-cup. It is then hurled, seething, into the face of (if I may use the expression) a thirsting idol and given him to drink as a ruthless beast. And amid the delights of the spectators, the death of certain victims is expended so that the bloody spectacle can teach others brutality. You would think that one's own private madness were not enough and that one had to learn more in public. (2) A wild beast is trained with gentle care so that it will, in turn, serve to punish a man and perform with greater fury before the spectators' eyes. A trained animal is given instructions; it would have perhaps been less ferocious, if its yet more cruel master had not trained it to act ferociously. (3) Of course, I say nothing of what idolatry further sanctions: how vain are the contests themselves, the quarreling over

1 Consus is said to have given Romulus the counsel to carry off the women, when the Sabines attended the games (*Consualia*) held in Consus' honor. See Tertullian, *Spect.* 5.5 (tr. Arbesmann, FC 40.60-61).

colors,[1] the vying with one another over different chariots, resound-
ing acclamations over mere marks of prestige, the rejoicing that one
horse was faster than another, the grieving that one ran too slow,
trying to reckon the age of a beast, becoming acquainted with the
consuls under whom the horses ran, ascertaining their different ages,
pinpointing their breed, recalling even their grandsires and great-
grandsires. (4) Isn't this whole matter a waste of time—or rather,
shameful and despicable! If you should ask such a man, who knows
by heart the entire line of a horse's pedigree and can rattle it off very
quickly and without a mistake, who were the parents of Christ, he
would not know, or if he does know, he is even more miserable.
Again, if I should ask him what road he took to get to that public
display, he will admit that he got there by way of brothels and the
naked bodies of prostitutes, wanton licentiousness, public vice, notorious lechery, and general contempt for all things. (5) Although I am
not upbraiding him for what he himself possibly may have done, he
has been a witness, nonetheless, to what must never be done and his
eyes, drawn by lust, are fixed on the public display of idolatry. He
would not hesitate, if he could, to take what is holy into the brothel
with him. He rushes over to the public display after dismissal from
the Lord's sacrifice, and still bearing with him, as is the custom, the
Eucharist, that faithless man has carried into the midst of the foul
bodies of prostitutes the sacred Body of the Lord. He has brought
down on his head greater damnation for the route by which he
arrived at that public display than for the pleasure derived therefrom.

Chapter 6

Permit me now to pass on to the brazen witticisms of the stage.[1] I
am ashamed to tell you what is said there. I am embarrased even to
expose what things take place—the artificial turnings of the plots,

1 Cf. Tertullian, *Spect.* 9.5 (tr. Arbesmann, FC. 40.72). Red and white were
   the original colors.

1 Cf. Cyprian, *To Donatus* 8 (tr. R. J. Deferrari, FC 36.13-14).

the deceits of adulterers, the immoralities of women, the scurrilous jokes, the sordid parasites, even the toga-clad heads of households, at times simply silly, at other times morally disgusting—in all instances senseless, on certain counts shameless. (2) No man—regardless of his background or profession—is spared by the despicable tongue of these rogues. Yet everyone still frequents the theater. Indecorum, commonly encountered, evidently delights to know and to learn of vice. There is a general rush to that despicable brothel of public shame, to the teaching of obscenity. Nothing is done in private that is not learned in public. In the laws themselves one is taught to break the law. (3) What is a faithful Christian doing there, when he is not even allowed to think of evil? Why does one delight in representations of wantonness? Modesty is laid aside, and one grows presumptuously confident to commit greater crimes. When one is accustomed to see such things, one also learns to act accordingly. As for those unfortunate women who have been debased in the service of public lewdness, they find concealment in their very location. In hiding they alleviate their shameful behavior. They who prostitute their virtue are ashamed to be seen doing so. (4) But that public monstrosity takes place for all to see and surpasses the foulness of prostitutes. A method is sought whereby adultery may be committed with one's eyes! (5) An evil quite worthy of it is added to this infamy: a completely broken down human being, a man soft beyond effeminacy, devoted to the art of expressing words with his hands. Because of one single I-don't-know-what, neither man nor woman, the entire city is excited so that the legendary orgies of bygone ages are carried out with frenzied dancing. So true is it that what is not permissible is eagerly sought after that what time itself has obscured is again remembered and brought to light.

Chapter 7

Since the evils of the present day do not suffice to glut the sensuality of our times, recourse has to be had to the theatre where the aberrations of a past age are again presented. It is not permissible, I repeat, for faithful Christians to be present. It is absolutely unlawful even for these whom—to charm their ears—Greece sends everywhere to all who are instructed in her vain arts. (2) One person tries to imitate the harsh war cry of the trumpet. A second person by blowing with his breath into pipes modulates their lugubrious sounds. A third, accompanied with dancing and a man's melodious voice, strains with his breath—laboriously drawn from the viscera to the upper parts of his body—to play upon the small openings of pipes.[1] At times he represses the breath and bottles it up inside; and at other times he releases and forces it into the air by means of fixed apertures. He even labors actually to speak with his fingers by breaking down the sound into definite rhythmic patterns. He is ungrateful to his Maker who gave him a tongue. (3) Why should I even mention the wasted efforts of comedy and those senseless ravings of the tragic voice? Why mention the din made by the vibrating strings of instruments? Even if such things were not consecrated to idols, faithful Christians should not go there and look at them. Even if they were not sinful, their distinguishing characteristic is unspeakable vanity, unbefitting the faithful.

Chapter 8

Another dementia on the part of some participants in the games provides open occupation for idle men: the gladiator fattens his body to its own detriment so that it can either more vigorously cut another to pieces or take a beating itself. So the first victory is for the belly to hunger after food beyond human capacity—a disgraceful business that lays claim to the crown of gluttony. One's miserable face is hired out to be beaten so that one's more miserable belly can itself be fattened. (2) How revolting are those bouts! One man clings with indecent holds and embraces to another man who lies beneath him. In such a contest there may be a question as to who the winner is—modesty is always the loser. Look at the nude man who leaps your way! At another who strains to toss a bronze ball into the air. Such is the glory of folly. In short, do away with the spectator, and the emptiness of the games is quite evident. I have

1 In antiquity the double flute or oblique flute and the panpipe were in use.

repeatedly stated that faithful Christians must shun such vain, such pernicious, such sacrilegious spectacles. It is imperative that our eyes and ears be guarded from them. (3) We soon get accustomed to what we hear and more quickly still to what we see. Since man's mind is of itself inclined to sin, what will become of it if it is faced with living models of vice? The body of its nature tends quickly down—what will happen if it is deliberately aroused? You must turn the mind's attention away from such things.

Chapter 9

A Christian has, if he so wills, better spectacles; he has pleasures genuine and profitable to him, if he will but recollect himself. He has—not to mention those sights which he cannot contemplate yet—this beautiful world[1] to look at and admire. Let him look at the sunrise and sunset that keep alternating with each other to summon forth the days and nights. The moon's sphere with its waxings and wanings indicates for us the different periods of time. There are the glittering choruses of stars continuously twinkling from on high with extremely rapid movement. (2) Through their successive movements the parts of the whole year and the very days and nights with the intervals of the hours are marked off. The ponderous weight of the earth is counterbalanced by the mountains. There are the flowing streams with their springs and great expanses of sea with breakers and shorelines. In the meantime, the intermediate air remains uniform in a supreme harmony and extends itself in bonds of concord, animating all things because it is so rare. Sometimes it sheds driving rain from its heavy clouds; at other times, it brings back the fair weather once the clouds become scarce. All these different elements have their own inhabitants: there are birds in the air, fishes in the water, man on earth. (3) I contend that these and similar divine works should be the spectacles of faithful Christians. What playhouse constructed by human hands can be compared to works such as these? Playhouses can be constructed with huge masses of stone, but the mountain crests are higher. The paneled ceilings may glisten

1 See Novatian, *Trin.* 1.1-8, 8.1.

with gold, but are no match for the glorious splendor of the stars. Human works lose their wonder for the man who knows that he is a son of God. The man who has admiration for anything other than God loses some of his dignity.

Chapter 10

I maintain that a faithful Christian should occupy himself with the Sacred Scriptures.[1] There he will find spectacles that become his faith. He will see God creating this world of His[2] and enriching that wonderful creation with men and other living things.[3] He will be a spectator of a world in the midst of its sins; its well-deserved shipwreck, the just rewarded and the wicked punished;[4] the sea turned for the people into dry land;[5] and water taken from a rock for the people to drink.[6] He will behold entire harvests falling from the heavens,[7] harvests that knew no plough or threshing-floor. (2) He will look upon rivers whose currents have been held in check to provide a dry crossing.[8] He will, in some men, see faith in mortal combat with fire,[9] and religion that overcomes and tames wild animals.[10] He will even look with astonishment at souls that have been recalled from death itself.[11] Furthermore, he will contemplate truly admirable souls that have been brought back from the grave to reanimate completely consumed bodies.[12] (3) In all these things, he will see even a greater spectacle: the devil who had vanquished the whole world lying prone under Christ's feet. How beautiful is this spectacle, brethren, how joyful, how necessary: always to look upon

1 Cf. Tertullian, *Spect.* 29.1 (tr. Arbesmann, FC 40.103).
2 Cf. Gen. 1.
3 Cf. Gen. 2.7.
4 Cf. Gen. 6.5-8; 7.21-23.
5 Cf. Exod. 14.21-22.
6 Cf. Exod. 17.6.
7 Cf. Exod. 16.4.
8 Cf. Jos. 3.15-17.
9 Cf. Dan. 3.23.
10 Cf. Dan. 6.22; 1 Macc. 2.60.
11 Cf. 4 Kings (2 Kings) 4.35.
12 Cf. Ezek. 37.1-11.

one's hope and to gaze upon one's salvation! (4) Such a spectacle is seen even if vision is lost. This is a spectacle that neither praetor nor consul presents—only He alone who is before all things and above all things—nay from whom all things come—the Father of our Lord Jesus Christ. To Him be given praise and honor forever and ever. Goodbye, brethren, and may you fare well.

JEWISH FOODS

INTRODUCTION

HE FATHERS OF THE CHURCH developed biblical typology and used it against the Gnostics to vindicate the unity of the two Testaments, and, against the Jews, the superiority of the New. Among the writings of the anti-Jewish polemic which are important for typology, one must mention the so-called *Epistle of Barnabas* and St. Justin's *Dialogue with Trypho,* both of the second century; Tertullian's *Against the Jews,* St. Cyprian's *To Quirinus: Three Books of Testimonies,* Novatian's *Jewish Foods,* certain pseudo-Cyprianic writings of which the chief is *Mounts Sinai and Sion,* and the *Syriac Didascalia,* all of the third century; several *Tractates* of St. Zeno of Verona against the Jews (on circumcision and Exodus) and the *Demonstrations* of the Syrian Aphraates of the fourth century.[1]

In his *Jewish Foods* Novatian made use of the following sources: (a) The text of Leviticus 11 (cf. Deut. 14.3-20), which deals with the question of clean and unclean food and clean and unclean animals: the principal argument of his work; (b) Seneca, *Epistle* 122.6: for the condemnation of early drinkers (cf. *Jewish Foods* 6.6-7); (c) The *Epistle of Barnabas* 10; (d) Pseudo-Aristeas (cf. Eusebius of Caesarea, *Preparation for the Gospel* 8.9 [PG 21.626-36]).[2] The last two sources give an allegorical interpretation of the levitical prescriptions regarding clean and unclean foods and animals. These interpretations tally with those found in Novatian's *Jewish Foods.* Although Philo of Alexandria (*De plantatione* 43) had interpreted the animals as symbols of human passions, "no one prior to Novatian had given such extensive treatment to the topic," observes J. Quasten, "and he thus paved the way for the wholesale allegorization that prevailed in the art and literature of the Middle Ages."[3]

1 J. Daniélou, *From Shadows to Reality* (Westminster, Md., 1960) 1.
2 A. Casamassa, *Novaziano* (Dispense universitarie; Rome 1949) 207.
3 Quasten, *Patrology* 2.221-22.

The first part of *Jewish Foods* deals with the prescriptions regarding the foods of the Old Testament (chs. 2-3); the second part treats of the norm now in effect under the New Dispensation (chs. 4-7). In the introduction, Novatian mentions two former works against the Jews: "In these letters, I have demonstrated how completely ignorant they are of the true nature of circumcision and of the true nature of the Sabbath" (ch. 1.6). These works, also mentioned by Jerome,[4] are lost.

The laws and prescriptions of the Old Testament, Novatian holds, must be understood spiritually. In the state of original justice, man plucked his food from the trees; after the fall, he had to bend down to the soil to cultivate his food. Since he must now cultivate the entire world, not merely paradise, flesh meat was added to his diet. When the law distinguishes between clean and unclean animals, that does not "dishonor their Creator"(ch. 2.3, 15-16). Unclean animals are to be given an allegorical interpretation: they are symbols of human vices (ch. 3). Certain foods were declared unclean to restrain the intemperance of the people (ch. 4).

The shadows and figures of the Old Law have served their purpose; with the advent of Christ, "the end of the law,"[5] "all things are pure to the pure."[6] The new food of Christians is now something real, pure, holy; that is, an upright faith, and immaculate conscience, an innocent spirit (ch. 5). Now that the Gospel affords Christians greater liberty in their choice of foods, "one must not conclude that sensuality is permitted" (ch. 6.1). Christians must not partake of what has been offered to idols; even Jews abhorred such offerings (ch. 7).

From the introduction (ch. 1), we can surmise that Novatian had been forced into exile—probably during the persecution of Gallus (251-253), at the time Pope Cornelius was also exiled. Socrates, the historian of the fifth century, claims that Novatian died "in the reign of Valerian," that is, between 253 and 260.[7] Since Novatian wrote

---

4 *On Circumcision* and *On the Sabbath*; cf. Jerome, *De viris illustribus* 70.
5 Rom. 10.4.
6 Titus 1.15.
7 Socrates, *Historia ecclesiastica* 4.28.

his work on *Jewish Foods* during his exile, the date of composition falls in the period 253-260.[8]

The present translation is based on the critical text of G. Landgraf and C. Weyman in *Archiv für lateinische Lexikographie und Grammatik* 11 (1900) 221-49. However, the emendations of G. F. Diercks in his just-published edition (CCL 4) have been incorporated.

---

8 Still, other positions are plausible. Diercks, CCL 4.xii, presents the position of H.J. Vogt that the work precedes the Decian persecution but follows Novatian's ordination as priest.

SELECT BIBLIOGRAPHY

Texts:

Diercks, G. F. *Novatiani Opera . . .* (CCL 4) 79-101.

Landgraf, G. and Weyman, C. "Novatians Epistula de cibis Iudaicis," *Archiv für lateinische Lexikographie und Grammatik* 11 (1900) 221-49.

Translations:

Wallis, R. E. in *Ante-Nicene Christian Library* 13 (Edinburgh 1880) 382-95; *The Ante-Nicene Fathers* 5 (New York 1899) 645-50.

Secondary Sources:

Quasten, J. *Patrology* 2. 219-23.

Weyman, C. "Novatian und Seneca über den Frühtrunk," *Philologus* 52 (1893) 728-30.

Wilmart, A. "Un manuscrit du *De cibis* et des oeuvres de Lucifer," *Revue Bénédictine* 33 (1921) 124-35.

CONTENTS

JEWISH FOODS

Chapter 1

Novatian sends his greetings to the people who stand firm in the Gospel.[1]

 ARDENTLY LONG, MOST HOLY BRETHREN, for the day when I can receive your letters and news and I number it among the happiest and most cherished of days. For now what else is there that can possibly be more pleasing to me? Nevertheless, I do not consider that day less precious, or less one to be reckoned among the golden days, when I can send back to you similar sentiments of the love I owe you and with equal longing write to you. (2) Nothing, most holy brethren, holds me shackled with fetters so strong, nothing troubles and vexes me with such prickings of anxiety and solicitude as the fear that you should think that my absence has caused you any inconvenience whatever. I endeavor to alleviate this situation when I strive to make myself present to you by means of my frequent letters. (3) Although the demands of my office and the position I have assumed and the very character of the ministry placed on my shoulders make it imperative that I engage in letter writing, nevertheless, you greatly intensify this obligation of mine when you compel me to answer your many letters. And inclined as I am to these habitual demonstrations of affection, you press me the more when you show that you are always remaining steadfast in the Gospel.[2] (4) By my letters to you, I do not so much instruct the well-informed[3] as stimulate those who are ready. Since you keep the Gospel unadulterated and free from all taint of erroneous doctrine and also enthusiastically defend

1 1 Cor. 15.1.
2 1 Cor. 15.1.
3 For Novatian's expression cf. Seneca, *Ep.* 94.11.

143

it, you do not need a man as teacher. Your accomplishments show that you are disciples of <Christ>.

I encourage you as you advance on your way,[4] I arouse you as you keep watch.[5] (5) I speak consoling words to you as you wrestle "against the spiritual forces of wickedness."[6] I urge you on as you strive "for the prize of the heavenly call in Christ."[7] After you have dashed to the ground and vanquished the sacrilegious invectives of the heretics and the idle fables of the Jews, hold fast to tradition alone and the teaching of Christ.[8] In so doing, you can deservedly lay claim to the authority of His Name. (6) I think that I have sufficiently indicated in two earlier letters how stiff-necked the Jews are and how alien they are from a true understanding of their law. In these letters, I have demonstrated how completely ignorant they are of the true nature of circumcision and of the true nature of the Sabbath.[9] Their blindness envelops them more and more. (7) In this letter I want to say something briefly concerning their foods also. For they believe, because of their foods, that they alone are holy and that all others are defiled.[10]

Chapter 2

I must, from the outset, insist that the Law is spiritual.[1] If the Jews deny that it is spiritual, they are certainly blaspheming. If they want to avoid blasphemy and acknowledge that it is spritual, then let them take it in a spiritual sense. Divine things must be taken in a divine manner, and holy things must be regarded in a holy manner.

4 Cf. Gal. 5.7.
5 Cf. Matt. 26.41.
6 Eph. 6.12.
7 Phil. 3.14.
8 That is, the Rule of Faith; cf. *Trin.* 1.
9 Cf. Jerome, *De viris illustribus* 70. Cf. above, Intr. at n. 4; General Intr. at n. 35.
10 Cf. Gregory of Elvira, *Tractatus Origenis* 13, lines 59-61 (ed. Bulhart, CCL 69.100).

1 Cf. Rom. 7.14.

(2) He falls into grave error who gives a human and worldly meaning to sacred and spiritual writings. Be wary of such a pitfall. (3) This pitfall can be avoided if God's precepts are treated in such a way that they harmonize with God and do not obscure His majesty but reveal it and do not diminish His authority by being taken inappropriately. This will come about if, when some things are called unclean, their creation would dishonor their Creator.

(4) If He disapproves of what He has made, He will seem to have condemned His own works—works He had approved of as good.[2] In both acts He will be branded so as to appear capricious, as some heretics will have it. Accordingly, either He blessed works that were not clean, or He blessed[3] works because they were both clean and good but later rejected them as not good since in fact they were not clean. (5) If this Jewish teaching persists, controversy over this irregularity will last forever. We must make every effort to lop off this teaching so that, in rejecting what they irregularly handed down, we may again attribute to God a suitable arrangement of His works and to God's law a spiritual and fitting interpretation.

(6) But let me commence from the beginning, as I should. Man's first food[4] was solely fruit, and produce from trees.[5] Man's guilt subsequently introduced the use of bread.[6] The posture of his body shows forth the state of his conscience. As long as man's conscience did not reproach him, innocence raised him up toward the heavens to pluck his food from the trees. Once sin had been committed, it bowed man down to the soil of the earth to get grain. (7) Still later, the use of meat was added.[7] Divine benevolence has provided human needs with adequate kinds of foods to suit every age. A more delicate food was needed to sustain young and tender bodies. This delicate food was confected <not> without labor for the correction <of the impious>. If the labor imposed on them did not recall to mind innocence lost, free rein would be given to sin again. (8) Hearty flesh

---

2 Cf. Gen. 1.10, 12.
3 Gen. 1.28.
4 Cf. Tertullian, *De ieiunio* 4 (tr. by S. Thelwall, *Ante-Nicene Fathers* 4.104).
5 Cf. Gen. 1.29; Vergil, *Georgics* 1.55.
6 Cf. Gen. 3.19.
7 Cf. Gen. 9.3.

meat is proffered to men who must now cultivate the entire world and not merely take care of paradise. Since the cultivation of the land requires so much exertion, the human body had to be sustained with something more substantial. (9) These things, as I previously stated, came about by divine favor and arrangement. If too little food were given to the hale and hardy, they would be weakened thereby and too exhausted for work. If too much food were forced upon the youthful, they would be burdened beyond their capacity and could not endure it.

(10) When the Law supervened, it made a distinction among flesh meats.[8] It set apart and assigned for use some animals as being clean; others were outlawed as being not clean and sure to defile their consumers.[9] (11) Under the Law, cloven-hoofed ruminants have the nature of clean animals. Animals that have neither or only one of these characteristics are unclean.[10] (12) With regard to aquatic animals, only those that are covered with scales and equipped with fins are considered clean. All others are not clean.[11] (13) The Law also sets down definite criteria whereby birds are judged clean or loathsome.[12] (14) Thus the Law has called into play a very great subtlety in making a division among animals.

The ancient ordinance had included all living things under one form of blessing.[13] (15) What shall we say? Are those animals, therefore, unclean—for what else is it to be not clean? —that the Law has withdrawn from use as food? What then? Do we reach the conclusion already mentioned? Is God, then, the Creator of things not clean? Will the defect in created things dishonor their Maker as producing things not clean? (16) To make such a statement is sheer madness. It would make God the author of uncleanness. The Divine Majesty would stand charged with the offense of making loathsome

---

8 Cf. Lev. 11; Deut. 14.3-21.
9 For the preceding two sentences, cf. Isidore of Seville, *Quaestiones in Leviticum* 9.1 (PL 83.325BC); quoted from Isid. by Ps.-Beda, *In Levit.* 11 (PL 91.345BC).
10 Cf. Lev. 11.3-4; Deut. 14.6-7.
11 Cf. Lev. 11.9-12; Deut. 14.9-10.
12 Cf. Lev. 11.13-19; Deut. 14.11-18.
13 Cf. Gen. 1.22.

things. Above all, remember that God Himself stated that these things were "very good"[14] and, because they were good, He gave them His blessing to increase and multiply.[15] (17) Furthermore, the Creator commanded Noah to save living things—for their off-spring—in his ark. That they were to be closely safeguarded is sufficient proof of their usefulness.[16] Their usefulness is evidence of their goodness. Even on that occasion, the distinction[17] was made. The creation of those unclean things could have been completely terminated if their uncleanness had necessitated their extermination.

Chapter 3

Since I have already demonstrated on the authority of the Apostle that this Law is spiritual,[1] it must be taken in a spiritual sense so that a heavenly and a true notion of the Law may be given. First, one must firmly keep in mind that what God has created is clean.[2] Creation is irreproachable because it has God's stamp of approval. To find fault with creation is to find fault with its Author. (2) The children of Israel received the Law so that they might profit by it and practice virtue again. Their forefathers had blessed them with good morals which they, in turn, lost in Egypt among a barbarous people. (3) Finally, the Ten Commandments, given to them on tablets, taught them nothing new. They merely called attention to what had been forgotten, so that the Law might rekindle in them, as it were, a smoldering justice. (4) They could make progress with the realization that man, above all, must avoid defects that were condemned by the Law even in animals. For when an irrational animal is

---

14 Gen. 1.31.
15 Gen. 1.22.
16 Cf. Gen. 7.2-3.
17 Namely, between clean and unclean animals (cf. Gen. 7.2). This distinction seems to indicate that people ate flesh meat before the flood.

---

1 Cf. Rom. 7.14.
2 For this and the following four sentences, cf. Isid., *op. cit.* 9.1 (PL 83.325BC); a part quoted from Isid. by Hrabanus Maurus, *Expositio in Levit.* 3.1 (PL 108.352C).

rejected on account of some one thing, that thing is the more condemned in man, who is rational. If what an animal has from its own nature is stigmatized as a sort of defilement, then the same thing is more blameworthy when found in man against his nature. (5) Accordingly, fault was found with animals, so that man might improve himself: men with like defects were considered equal to brutes.[3] In this way, animals are not condemned through any fault of their Creator, and men are instructed by mere brutes to return to the immaculate nature of their own creation.

Let us consider how the Law distinguishes between clean and not clean: Clean animals, it states, chew the cud and divide the hoof; the unclean do neither, or only one of the two.[4] The same Creator made and blessed all these creatures.[5] (6) Therefore I regard the creation of both as clean, because their Creator is holy and created things are without fault because they are simply what they were created to be. A perverted will—never nature—always assumes the burden of guilt. (7) Then, what is it all about? In animals we find portrayed human traits, deeds, and acts of will that determine whether men are clean or unclean.[6] Men are clean if they ruminate, that is if they always have the divine commandments in their mouth as a kind of food.[7] (8) They divide the hoof if they follow their path throughout life with a step steady in innocence, justice, and all virtues.[8] The gait of the cloven-hoofed is always firm. A place that is slippery for one part of the hoof is steadied by the support <of the other> so that one can keep his footing. (9) The unclean are those that do neither of these things. Their step is not firm in the way of the virtues, and the food of the divine precepts is not worn down in the mouth by any [rumination].

(10) They are also not clean who do merely one of the two,

3 For this sentence, cf. Isid., *op. cit.* 9.3 (PL 83.325CD).

4 Cf. Lev. 11.3-4; Deut. 14.6-7.

5 Cf. Gen. 1.22.

6 See the *Epistle of Barnabas* 10 (tr. by J. A. Kleist, ACW 6.51-53).

7 Cf. Deut. 8.3; Matt. 4.4; Irenaeus, *Adversus haereses* 5.8.3 (PG 7.1143AB; Sources Chrétiennes 153.100-101); Origen (tr. Rufinus), *In Levit. hom.* 7.6 (PL 12.415C-416AB; GCS 29.389).

8 For the preceding four sentences, cf. Isid., *op. cit.* 9.4 (PL 83.326CD); quoted from Isid. by Ps.-Beda, *In Levit.* 11 (PL 91.345BC).

because they are deficient in one and not perfect in both. (11) There
are the following: the faithful, who do both and are clean; the Jews
and heretics, who do only one of the two and are defiled; the
pagans, who do neither of these things and are, therefore, unclean.
(12) By having recourse to animals, the Law places before men some
sort of mirror, so to speak, of human life, wherein they may see
their own actions reflected, so that whatever vicious acts are committed against nature in man's case may receive greater condemnation, especially when these things naturally ordained in animals are
reproved.

(13) When fish with rough scales are considered clean,[9] men with
austere, rough, unpolished, steadfast, and grave traits are commended; fish without scales are unclean[10] because loose, fickle, in-
sincere, and effeminate traits are censured. (14) What does the Law
mean when it states: "You shall not eat the camel"?[11] From the
example of an animal, it censures an unruly life and one distorted
by disorders.[12] (15) What does the Law mean when it forbids one to
partake of the flesh of swine?[13] It condemns, you can be sure, a
foul and filthy life—one that delights in sordid vices by placing its
supreme good, not in nobility of spirit, but in the flesh alone. (16)
What does the Law want to indicate when it forbids the hare?[14] It
denounces effeminate men.[15] (17) Who would use as food the flesh
of the weasel?[16] In it the Law condemns theft.

(18) Who would dare partake of the skink? The Law abhors a
capricious and fickle life. (19) Who would eat the newt? The Law detests aberrations <of the mind. (20) Who would dare partake of the
hawk, the kite, or the eagle?[17] The Law hates marauders and those who
live by violence. (21) Who does not loathe the vulture?> The Law exe-

9 Cf. Lev. 11.9; Deut. 14.9.
10 Cf. Lev. 11.10-12; Deut. 14.10.
11 Cf. Lev. 11.4; Deut. 14.7.
12 Cf. Gregory of Elvira, *Tract. Orig.* 14, line 100 (CCL 69.109).
13 Cf. Lev. 11.7; Deut. 14.8.
14 Cf. Lev. 11.6; Deut. 14.7.
15 Cf. Gregory of Elvira, *op. cit.* 10, line 272 (CCL 69.83).
16 Cf. Lev. 11.29-30.
17 Cf. Lev. 11.13-14, 16; Deut. 14.12-13, 15.

crates those who look for booty in someone else's death. (22) Who would eat the crow? The Law detests immoral and shady intentions. (23) When the Law prohibits the ostrich,[18] it disapproves of intemperance. When it condemns the nightjar, it hates those who shun the light of truth. When it bands the swan, it loathes stiff-necked pride. When it excludes the heron, it dislikes a garrulous and undisciplined tongue. When it detests the bat,[19] it condemns those who seek out the darkness of error that is like night. (24) The Law execrates the aforementioned and similar characteristics in animals. Since the animals, however, are born with such characteristics, they are without reproach. Conversely, such qualities are reprehensible in man, who was not created with them but seeks after them contrary to his nature, through the exercise of his own error.[20]

Chapter 4

That is how matters stand presently. There are, however, additional reasons why the Jews were deprived of many different kinds of foods. To bring this about, many foods were said to be unclean, not to condemn the foods, but to restrain the Jews. (2) It was fitting that the people who were chosen to serve God should possess the virtues of frugality and moderation in eating, qualities which have a certain affinity with religion, or rather, are, so to speak, consanguineous and cognate with it for sensuality is an enemy of holiness. If modesty is not spared, will religion be? (3) Sensuality leaves no room for the fear of God since it is completely dominated by sensual gratifications, seeking only to glut its inordinate desires. Once unbridled, sensuality flourishes; it brazenly devours its patrimony,[1] like fire that receives more fuel, or like a torrent cascading from the mountain-peaks that not only sweeps over all barriers, but

18 Latin *passer;* Novatian has in mind here the *passer marinus,* the ostrich (called *marinus* because brought from a distance by sea [*mare*]).
19 Lev. 11.14-19; Deut. 14.13-18.
20 For the last two paragraphs of this chapter (sections 13-24), cf. Isid., *op. cit.* 9.6-10 (PL 83.326A-C); quoted from Isid. by Ps.-Beda, *In Levit.* 11 (PL 91.345D-346A) and by Hrab. Maur., *loc. cit.* (PL 108.358AB).

1 Cf. Seneca, *Dial.* 12 (*Ad Helviam de consolatione*) 14.2.

also drags them along to the destruction of others. (4) These remedies were sought to check the intemperance of the people in order that, as sensuality was constrained, virtue might flourish. (5) Since they dared to prefer the bitterest of Egyptian foods[2] to the heavenly food of manna and preferred the succulent meats of their hostile masters to their own freedom,[3] did they deserve anything else than to have their joy in foods curtailed? They truly deserved to bear the brand of the slavery they had longed for, since a better food—the food of the free—displeased them so.

Chapter 5

There was indeed a time long ago in which attention was to be paid to these shadows and figures prescribing abstinence from foods pronounced good in their creation but forbidden by the Law. (2) When "Christ, the consummation of the Law"[1] came, He cleared up all the ambiguities of the Law ⟨and⟩ all those things which antiquity had shrouded in mystery. That distinguished teacher and heavenly doctor and author of consummate truth states: "To all who are pure themselves, everything is pure; but to those who have been corrupted and lack faith, nothing can be pure—the corruption is both in their minds and in their consciences."[2] (3) Likewise, in another passage, he states: "For every creature of God is good, and nothing is to be rejected that is accepted with thanksgiving. For it is sanctified by the word of God and prayer."[3] (4) And again he states elsewhere: "Now the Spirit expressly says that in later times some

2 Aphraates (cf. Intr. at n. 1) gives a striking account of the origins of the dietary laws. He thinks these laws were instituted only after the Hebrews' contact with the Egyptians, who worshipped animals. See J. Neusner, "The Jewish-Christian Argument in Fourth-Century Iran: Aphrahat on Circumcision, The Sabbath, and The Dietary Laws," *Journal of Ecumenical Studies* 7 (1970) 294-98.

3 Exod. 16.3.

1 Rom. 10.4.

2 Titus 1.15. For the contents of ch. 5.1-2, cf. Isid., *op. cit.* 9.11 (PL 83.326D-327A).

3 1 Tim. 4.4-5.

will depart from the faith, giving heed to deceitful spirits and doctrines of devils, speaking lies hypocritically, and having their conscience branded. They will forbid marriage, and [will enjoin] abstinence from foods which God has created to be partaken of with
thanksgiving by the faithful and by those who know God."[4] (5) In
another passage, he states: "Do not hesitate to eat anything that is
sold in the market: there is no need to raise questions."[5]

(6) Accordingly, it is evident that all these foods enjoy again the
blessings they received at their creation, now that the Law has
ended,[6] and that we must not return to the legal prohibition of
foods commanded for certain reasons, and which evangelical liberty,
setting us free from its bondage,[7] has now discontinued. (7) The
Apostle exclaims: "Food and drink is not good, but righteousness
and peace and joy."[8] (8) In another passage, he states: "Food for
the belly and the belly for the body, but God will destroy both the
one and the other. Now the body is not for immorality, but for the
Lord, and the Lord for the body."[9] (9) God is not worshipped by
the belly nor by foods, which the Lord says will perish and are
discharged into the privy in accordance with the natural law of
life.[10] The man who worships God with foods is almost like one who
has God as his belly.[11]

(10) True and holy and pure food, I maintain, is an upright faith,
immaculate conscience, and innocent spirit. (11) Whoever partakes
of food in this manner eats with Christ. One who dines thus is a
guest of God. This is the food of angels, the banquet which makes
martyrs. (12) Accordingly, we have the pronouncement of the Law:
"Not by bread alone does man live, but by every word that comes
forth from the mouth of the Lord."[12] (13) Christ says: "My food is

4 1 Tim. 4.1-3.
5 1 Cor. 10.25.
6 Cf. Rom. 10.4.
7 Cf. Gal. 4.
8 Rom. 14.17.
9 1 Cor. 6.13.
10 Cf. Matt. 15.17; Mark 7.19.
11 Cf. Phil. 3.19.
12 Deut. 8.3; Matt. 4.4.

to do the will of the one who sent Me, and to complete His work." [13]
(14) And again he says: "You seek Me, not because you have seen
signs, but because you have eaten of my loaves and have been filled. Do
not labor for the food that perishes but for that which endures unto
life everlasting, that which the Son of Man will give you. For upon
Him the Father, God Himself, has set His seal." [14]

(15) I maintain that God is worshipped by righteousness, and
moderation, and the other virtues. (16) Zechariah also states: "And
when you eat or drink, do you not yourselves eat or drink? " [15] He
wants to say that food and drink are things proper to man, not to
God, because God is not made of flesh. God is not pleased by flesh
meat nor is He intent upon enjoying the pleasure of our foods. (17)
God only delights in our faith, our innocence, our truthfulness,
those virtues of ours which dwell in the soul, not the stomach. Fear
of God and heavenly awe, not earthly perishable food, obtain these
virtues for us. (18) With reason does the Apostle rebuke those who
are slaves to the superstitions pertaining to angels, "inflated with
their fleshly outlook, not clinging to Christ, who is the head, by
whom the whole body is fitted together by joints, and fastened
together and united by mutual members in the bond of love to reach
full growth in the Lord." [16] They prefer to follow the admonition:
"Do not touch, nor handle" [17] things that indeed seem to have a
show of religion because the body is treated severely. [18] Yet there is
in them no increase at all of righteousness in that we are recalled by
a self-imposed slavery to the rudiments [19] to which we are dead
through baptism.

13 John 4.34.
14 John 6.26-27.
15 Zech. 7.6.
16 Col. 2.18-19; cf. 3.14.
17 Col. 2.21.
18 Cf. Col. 2.23.
19 Cf. Col. 2.20.

Chapter 6

Since certain privileges are granted regarding foods, one must not be quick to conclude that sensuality is permitted, or that moderation in food and drink is abolished because the Gospel now treats us with more liberality. (2) All this, I repeat, is not a catering to one's appetite for food; it merely demonstrates the inner nature of foods. It indicates one's rights, not the way to insatiable voraciousness; it gives an explanation of the law. (3) Nothing has checked intemperance like the Gospel, nor has anyone given stricter laws against gluttony than Christ, of whom one reads that He declared the poor, blessed; the hungry and the thirsty, happy.[1] He said that the wealthy are wretched because they obey the dictates of the belly and of gluttony. The mother of sensuous pleasures never abandons them and they are always in servitude to her. They consider it a proof of real happiness when they have the largest possible appetite; but the fact is that, in so doing, they succeed in obtaining less than they crave. (4) When Christ preferred Lazarus, who was starving to death and covered with sores amid the dogs, to the rich man, He restrained with these examples the executioners of salvation, namely the belly and the gullet.[2]

(5) The Apostles also gave us the law of frugality and moderation, when he stated: "If we have food and clothing we are content with these."[3] He knew full well that what he had written would be of little profit unless he also gave himself as a model of what he had written, aptly subjoining that covetousness is the root of all evils;[4] for covetousness follows its forerunner, profligacy. Whatever the latter dissipates through vice, the former replaces by theft. We have a vicious circle of wrongdoing: profligacy expends again, what covetousness has accumulated. (6) Nor are there wanting at the present time those who merely play the role of Christian, but who are really models and proponents of intemperance. Their disorderly

1 Cf. Matt. 5.3, 6.
2 Cf. Luke 16.19 ff.
3 1 Tim. 6.8.
4 Cf. 1 Tim. 6.10.

conduct has reached the point where they do not nesitate to drink in the early morning, even though they are fasting. They do not think it Christian to drink after partaking of food, unless the wines poured into empty and vacant veins have been swallowed immediately after sleep. Drinkers seem to relish less the wines they have ingested if the wines are mixed with food.[5] (7) You are looking at a new breed: people who are still fasting but already intoxicated. They do not rush to the tavern, rather they carry the tavern about with them. If one of them greets anyone, he does not give a kiss but proposes a toast. What can these people possibly do after partaking of food, when they are already intoxicated when they first partake of the day's first food? In what condition will the setting sun find these people when the rising sun beholds them besotted with wine?

(8) But what must be detested is not to be reckoned an example for us. We should choose only the things that improve our soul and, although in the Gospel the use of foods is granted to us in every respect, one must realize that the use of these foods is given to us, however, with the law of frugality and moderation. (9) These virtues are very becoming to the faithful who are about to pray to God and to give Him thanks both by day and night. How can they possibly do either, if the mind is overcome by food and wine and is unable to shake off heavy sleep and the heavy weight on the breast?

Chapter 7

But concerning the use of foods one must be especially on his guard and not think for a moment that freedom has also been granted to partake of what has been offered to idols. If we have regard only to God's creation every food is clean; but once it has been offered to demons, it is defiled for God, insofar as it is offered to idols.[1] (2) As soon as this has been done, the food belongs not to God, but to an idol. When this is taken as food, it nourishes the one who partakes of it for the devil, not for God, and makes him a

5 Seneca, *Ep.* 122.6.

1 For ch. 7.1-2, cf. Isid., *op. cit.* 9.12 (PL 83.327A).

table-companion of an idol, not of Christ, as the Jews also rightly hold.[2]

Now that we understand the nature of Jewish foods, the reason for the Law, and the condescensions of Evangelical grace, and now that we have observed the rigors of temperance and repudiated the uncleanness of what has been offered to idols, let us observe the Rule of Truth in all things and give thanks to God through Jesus Christ, His Son, our Lord, to whom be praise, honor, and glory forever.

2 Cf. 1 Cor. 10.20-21.

IN PRAISE OF PURITY

INTRODUCTION

OVATIAN'S WORK *In Praise of Purity (De bono pudicitiae)* is revealed in its opening chapter as a pastoral letter, but one written from a distance, since, as in *The Spectacles* and *Jewish Foods,* the bishop-author is absent from his flock. His theme is purity (or chastity),[1] whose safeguard is what we today call "modesty." The work shows close imitation of three treatises of Tertullian—*Purity (De pudicitia), The Dress of Women (De cultu feminarum), The Veiling of Virgins (De virginibus velandis)*—as well as *The Dress of Virgins (De habitu virginum)* of Cyprian.[2]

Novatian exhorts his followers to cultivate this virtue because they are temples of the Lord, members of Christ, and the dwelling-place of the Holy Spirit (ch. 2). To place the virtue of purity in greater relief, the author describes the sad effects of impurity (ch. 3). There are three degrees of purity: virginity, continence, and faithfulness to the marriage bond; this virtue is, however, God's gift (ch. 4). The precept to observe conjugal purity is ancient, because it "originated with man himself" (ch. 5), but it was restored to its pristine splendor by Christ (ch. 6). Virginity and continence transcend every law and render one superior to the angels (ch. 7). Joseph in Egypt (ch. 8) and Susanna (ch. 9) are shining examples of purity in Holy Scripture; chapter 10 describes their struggles and final recompense. The greatest victory for a Christian is to conquer his own unruly passions (ch. 11). The concluding chapters (12-14) deal with the dangers to purity and the means one must take to preserve it.

In all the manuscripts but one the work is anonymous. MS lat. 1658 (Z) of the Paris Bibliothèque Nationale shows the following at

1 See W. Le Saint, ACW 28.189.
2 Quasten, *Patrology* 2.226.

the end of the treatise: "Caecilii Cypriani de pudicitia explicit,"[3] thus reflecting an erroneous attribution that originated at a late date (14th-15th century). Nothing in fact points to Cyprian's authorship, and neither the deacon Pontius in his life of Cyprian[4] not St. Augustine in several sermons on Cyprian[5] mentions the work.[6] Attribution to the true author, Novatian, dates from *ca.* 1900 and is based on the internal evidence alone. Not only does Novatian's style appear here in its best features—antithetic force, varied diction, and rhythm[7]—but the opening reveals, as we have seen, the same relation between author and addressees that is found in two other works of Novatian. The date of composition falls within the period 253-260, for the reasons already given for *The Spectacles* and *Jewish Foods.*[8] Passages of the *De bono pudicitiae* were used in the *Tractatus Origenis* of Gregory of Elvira (died after 392),[9] and somewhat earlier by Bishop Zeno of Verona.[10]

The first printing is that of Richard Paffroet, Deventer (Holland), 1477, whose text, with some minor corrections, was taken over by Erasmus, Bâle 1520.[11] The text used for the present translation is that edited by W. Hartel (Vienna 1871), but full use has been made of the recent critical study of G. F. Diercks and of his just-published edition, CCL 4 (see Select Bibliography), where for the first time the work is joined to the other writings of Novatian.

3 See the critical apparatus of Hartel and Diercks.
4 *Vita Cypriani* 7 (CSEL 3.3.xcvii f.; trans. Müller-Deferrari, FC 15.3-24).
5 *Sermones* 309-13 (PL 38) and those published by G. Morin in *Miscellanea Agostiniana* 1 (Rome 1930) listed *ibid.* p. 844 (Nos. 121-26). The fact that Augustine does not refer to any such work as the *De bono pudicitiae* in Serm. Guelf. 26.2 (Morin, *op. cit.* 528-31; PL Suppl. 2.610) is especially indicative.
6 Casamassa, *Novaziano* (Dispense universitarie; Rome 1949) 223.
7 For a brief survey of the question of the authorship of the *De bono pudicitiae,* see B. Melin, *Studia in Corpus Cypr.* (Uppsala 1946) 6-9; 208-9.
8 For Vogt's earlier dating, see Diercks, CCL 4.xiii.
9 V. Bulhart, *Gregorii Iliberritani episcopi quae supersunt* (CCL 69) 406, Index scriptorum, s.v. Ps.-Cypr., *De bono pudicitiae.* All are noted below. See above, *Trinity* ch.5 n.1.
10 In his sermon *De pudicitia* (ed. B. Löfstedt, CCL 22).
11 G. F. Diercks, "Some Critical Notes on Novatian's De Bono Pudicitiae...," *Vigiliae Christianae* 25 (1971) 122.

SELECT BIBLIOGRAPHY

Texts:

Diercks, G. F. *Novatiani opera . . .* (CCL 4) 103-27.
Hartel, W. S. *Thasci Caecilii Cypriani opera omnia,* CSEL 3.3 (1871) 13-25.
Migne, J.-P. *Patrologia latina* 4.819-27.

Translations:

Malarkey, Sr. Mary Augustine, O. P. *Novatian's "De bono pudicitiae": A Translation with Introduction, Notes, and Commentary* [unpublished Catholic University of America M. A. dissertation] (Washington 1965). Unavailable to the present translator.
Wallis, R. E. *Ante-Nicene Christian Library* 13 (Edinburgh 1880) 253-63; *The Ante-Nicene Fathers* 5 (New York 1899) 587-92.

Secondary Sources:

Demmler, A. *Über den Verfasser der unter Cyprians Namen überlieferten Traktate "De bono pudicitiae" und "De spectaculis"* (Trübingen 1894).
Diercks, G. F. "Some Critical Notes on Novatian's De Bono Pudicitiae and the Anonymous Ad Novatianum," *Vigiliae Christianae* 25 (1971) 121-30.
Melin, B. *Studia in Corpus Cyprianeum* (Uppsala 1946).
Quasten, J. *Patrology* 2. 225-26.

CONTENTS

IN PRAISE OF PURITY

Chapter 1

OU KNOW VERY WELL that, when I was present with you,[1] I never neglected any part of my duty. I always endeavor with the Lord's help, especially by my daily explanations of the Gospels, to deepen your faith and knowledge. What else can be done to greater advantage in the Church of the Lord? (2) What can be more suited to the duties of a bishop than imparting knowledge of those divine truths which were promulgated and expounded by the Lord Himself, so that believers might attain the promised kingdom of heaven? Rest assured that I endeavor, despite my absence, to accomplish this pleasant daily task of my present office and mission. I strive by my letters to make myself present to you. (3) I admonish you in the faith, as is my custom, by the exhortations which I send you. I entreat you, therefore, to remain steadfast on the firm foundation of the Gospel and to stand armed against all the onslaughts of the devil. If I can count on you, I shall not feel absent from you. (4) Everything that is usefully expressed—sermons which either give an explanation or instil hope of the attainment of eternal life—eventually bears fruit, if the effort of the undertaking is aided by an abundance of divine grace. (5) We do not merely utter words, which come from the sacred sources of the Scriptures, but to these very words we join our prayers and supplications to the Lord. May He open to us, as well as to you, the treasures of His mysteries and grant us the strength to accomplish what we already know. There is greater danger of perdition when one knows the Lord's will and neglects to do His will.

1 Cf. Maximus of Turin, *Hom.* 30 and 33 *init.* (CCL 23.117, 128). This sentence, given in only one MS (Z), was first accepted by Diercks as the opening of the work.

Chapter 2

You know that I always encourage you in many of your undertakings [in compliance with the precepts] of divine counsel. (What
can be more pleasant, or mean more, to me than that you remain
perfect in the Lord? [1]) Above all, I admonish you to continue to
safeguard the bulwarks of purity. You know that you are the temple
of the Lord,[2] the members of Christ,[3] the dwelling place of the
Holy Spirit,[4] called to hope, consecrated to the faith, destined for
salvation, sons of God, brothers of Christ, and consorts of the Holy
Spirit. You no longer are debtors to the flesh[5] because you have
been reborn of water.[6] (2) May purity, then—that purity which goes
above and beyond the will and which we should will always to
possess—be also given to us for the sake of redemption, so that what
has been consecrated by Christ cannot be corrupted. If the Apostle
states that the Church is the bride of Christ,[7] I ask you now to
reflect just what purity is required of you, when the Church herself
is given in marriage as a virgin bride. (3) If I did not propose to
admonish you briefly, I could sing quite at length and rather exu-
berantly the praises of purity. I have deemed it unnecessary, however, to praise it at greater length among its devotees. You are an
ornament to purity while you possess it and, through exercising it,
you pour forth its praise. You are purity's ornament while also it is
yours, each mutually enriching one another. (4) It affords you the
discipline of wholesome morality; you devote to it the ministry of
holy works. On the one hand, you have demonstrated precisely
what, and how much, purity can accomplish. On the other hand,
purity indicates to you and teaches you what you aspire after—the
combined blessings of precept and actual practice, so that nothing be

---

1 Cf. Eph. 6.13.
2 Cf. 1 Cor. 3.16; 2 Cor. 6.16.
3 Cf. 1 Cor. 6.15.
4 Cf. 1 Cor. 6.19.
5 Cf. John 1.13; Rom. 8.12.
6 Here reappears the leading idea of Novatian's *Spectacles:* it is not sufficient
   to renounce paganism at baptism; the religion of Christ must pervade our
   daily life.
7 2 Cor. 11.2; Eph. 5.23.

wanting. Such would be the case if either principle fell short of deeds, or deeds of principle.

Chapter 3

Purity does honor to the body and is an ornament of virtue. It sanctifies both sexes and is the bond of marriage.[1] Purity guarantees parentage, defends modesty, and is a font of chastity. Purity brings peace to our homes and crowns harmony. Purity is full of concern to please no one but itself. Purity is always modest because it is the mother of innocence. Purity's sole adornment is modesty. The displeasure of the wicked is a sure guarantee of its beauty. Purity seeks no ornament: it is its own splendor. (2) It commends us to the Lord, unites us to Christ, expunges from our members all unlawful fomentations of desire, and brings peace to our bodies. Purity is itself blessed and makes those blessed with whom it deigns to dwell. Nor can even they who do not possess it find fault with it. It is revered even by its enemies. For they admire it the more who are unable to take it by storm. (3) This virtue is always esteemed in men and is earnestly to be sought after by women. Its adversary, impurity, must always be abhorred. It makes lewd sport of its victims, sparing neither bodies nor souls. (4) For once impurity has mastered one's moral control, it bends the entire man under the yoke of its wantonness. Initially, it is alluring, so that it may work more havoc by its very attraction. Impurity is the foe of continence. It consumes one's property as well as one's modesty. The insidious madness of lust not infrequently ends in bloodshed. It sets a good conscience afire. Impurity is the mother of impenitence, the ruin of one's better years and a stigma on one's lineage. It violates fidelity to one's own blood and family. It forces its own children upon the affections of strangers and places the child of an unknown and undesirable background in the wills and testaments of other people. (5) Impurity very often lusts without regard to sex, for it does not contain itself within what is permitted. It thinks itself unsatisfied unless it searches out and procures for itself even from the bodies of men, not simply a new pleasure, but, from men,

1 Cf. Tertullian, *On Purity* 1.1 (tr. by W.P. Le Saint, ACW 28.52).

through men, extraordinary and revolting monstrosities against nature itself.

Chapter 4

Purity holds first place among virgins, second place among those who exercise continence, third place among the married. Yet purity, with its several degrees, is truly glorious in all three classes. (2) For it is indeed praiseworthy to keep one's marriage vow amid so many hostile attacks of the flesh. Furthermore, it is more virtuous (since even lawful things are renounced) to set down certain restrictions in marriage regarding continence. (3) It is a token of truly admirable virtue to maintain one's purity of life from birth and to maintain oneself in the purity of an infant throughout the whole of one's life, even to old age, save only that it is a greater blessing never to have known the seductive demands of the flesh; just as it is a token of virtue to have vanquished its allurements, once they have been experienced. Nevertheless, one must realize that even this virtue is God's gift, though it manifests itself in one's members.

Chapter 5

Brethren, the precepts of purity are ancient. Why do I say ancient? Because they originated with the human race itself. (2) For woman was brought forth from man that she can know no other except him; and woman is given back to man so that, when what had been taken out of him is restored to him,[1] he may not seek for anything belonging to another. (3) Thus Scripture states: "And the two shall be but one flesh"[2] so that what was once one, may become one again, lest separation without reconciliation afford occasion for another partner. (4) For that reason, the Apostle also stated that the head of the woman is man[3] so that by the union of the two, he could commend [conjugal] purity. For just as the

1 Cf. Gen. 2.22.
2 Matt. 19.5; Mark 10.8.
3 Cf. 1 Cor. 11.3.

head of another is unsuitable for limbs <not>its own, so too, limbs not its own are unbecoming another's head. The head matches its own limbs and the limbs their own head, a natural bond uniting both in complete harmony, lest the pact of the divine covenant be shattered by some sort of discord arising from the division of members. (5) Furthermore, the text goes on to say that: "He who loves his own wife, loves himself. For no one ever hates his own flesh; on the contrary he nourishes and cherishes it, as Christ does the Church."[4] (6) This passage lays down the great law of charity along with conjugal purity, since husbands are to love their wives even as Christ loved the Church, and wives are to love their husbands as the Church loves Christ.

Chapter 6

Hence, when Christ was put to the test, He said that it was unlawful for a man to put away his wife, except for adultery.[1] Such was the esteem He had for conjugal purity. (2) Then there was the punitive sanction: Adulteresses you shall not permit to live.[2] (3) In like manner the Apostle states: "This is the will of God that you abstain from fornication."[3] (4) He also made that well-known statement: The members of Christ must not be joined to the members of a harlot.[4] (5) He who dares to trample under foot the precept of purity and practices the vices of the flesh is handed over to Satan for the destruction of the flesh.[5] (6) Adulterers for the same reason will not possess the kingdom of heaven.[6] He also states that every sin which a man commits is outside the body, but adultery alone sins against one's own body.[7] Since you are already cognizant of these

---

4 Eph. 5.28-29.

1 Cf. Matt. 5.32.
2 Cf. Lev. 20.10.
3 1 Thess. 4.3.
4 Cf. 1 Cor. 6.15.
5 Cf. 1 Cor. 5.5.
6 Cf. 1 Cor. 6.9.
7 Cf. 1 Cor. 6.18.

teachings and constantly live by them, I deem it unnecessary to bring to your attention the remaining authoritative directives of the commandments. (7) Although they are severe, one has no reason to complain of them. The adulterous man does not have an excuse: he either has or could have had—because it was permissible to marry—a wife.

Chapter 7

Married women are bound by the laws laid down for them, so that they cannot alienate themselves from them. Contrarily, virginity and continence are beyond all law. None of the laws of marriage appertain to virginity. Virginity transcends them all because of its sublimity, †if any depraved actions venturing to surmount the laws of men are attempted.†[1] (2) Virginity makes itself equal to the angels. If we examine the matter more carefully, we will find that virginity even outdoes the angels because it must struggle against flesh to gain mastery over a nature angels do not possess. (3) What is virginity, if not a magnificent contemplation of the afterlife? Virginity is not the exclusive possession of either sex. Virginity is a continuing infancy. Virginity means victory over pleasure. Virginity does not have children, but, what is more, holds them in disdain. It is not fruitful; so it does not suffer bereavement. Happy to escape the travail of childbirth, it is more fortunate to have been spared the deep distress of burying its own children. (4) What is virginity, but singular liberty? Virginity knows no husband for a master. It is free from all attachments, is not given up to nuptials, the world, or children. Virginity cannot fear persecution; from its vantage point of safety it can challenge it.

Chapter 8

Now that we have briefly expounded for you the precepts of purity, we would like to give a concrete example. Nothing is more encouraging than a concrete example. We will have no misgivings about such moral excellence, if what is commanded is also con-

---

1 Set off by Diercks as being corrupt or incomplete in the Latin.

firmed by examples. (2) Joseph[1] is our first example of purity. He
was an illustrious Hebrew youth by birth. His spotless life, however,
was his real title to nobility. Hated because of his dreams and sold
by his brothers to the Ishmaelites, he had come into the household
of an Egyptian. (3) By obedience, irreproachable conduct, and utterly faithful service, Joseph had earned the favor and good will of
his master. His appearance (that of a free man, though he was a
slave), which his youth and noble qualities had commended to all,
was observed, though not fittingly, by his master's wife. (4) Un-
observed, in a secluded area of the house, a hiding place suitable for
wicked acts, the incontinent, brazen woman thought she could overcome by means of blandishments and threats the young man's
purity. (5) Since he was endeavoring to get away from her, she
seized him by his clothes. Bewildered at the daring boldness of such
a heinous action, he left behind his very clothes. The purity of his
naked body furnished sufficient evidence of his integrity. The im-
pudent woman did not hesitate to add the foolhardiness of calumny to
the crime of immorality. (6) Rejection infuriated and crushed her.
Feigning grief, she charged the Hebrew youth with endeavoring to
inflict on her the very violence that she herself had tried to bring to
bear on him. (7) The passionate husband, in ignorance of the facts,
was greatly aroused by his wife's accusation. The chaste young man
was thrown into the lowest cell of the prison because he had refused
to stain his conscience with sin. (8) But purity was not alone in the
prison. God was with Joseph, and the evildoers were in his control
because he was innocent. (9) Furthermore, he interpreted certain
dreams because his spirit had been vigilant in time of trial. The
Lord[2] finally set him free. He who in a house of lower status had
done servant's work, and this amidst dangers, was now master of the

---

1 Cf. Gen. 39.7 ff.
2 What Novatian says next shows that he thought of Joseph receiving his
liberty from the Lord (at any rate, Gen. 41.14ff. shows that it was not
Potiphar, the master in question in Novatian's sentence, who freed Joseph).
Accordingly I read *Dominum* ("the Lord") rather than *dominum* ("his
master"), anticipated in this by the Battifol-Wilmart edition (Paris 1906, p.
46) of the relevant "Tractatus Origenis." Bulhart, however (see the following note), reads *dominum,* as does Diercks.

royal household free of any peril. His noble status was restored to him and he received—by the judgment of God, from whom he had merited it—the fruit of his purity and integrity.[3]

Chapter 9

The continence of women affords us a comparable example of chastity. (2) Scripture describes Susanna,[1] the daughter of Hilkiah and the wife of Joakim, as fair of face and fairer still in her character. Display did not commit her to [the cultivation of] her beauty, for she was without guile. Purity had adorned her and, with purity, nature alone. (3) Two of the elders fell desperately in love with her. They recklessly banished from their minds the fear of God and all thought of their advanced and fading years. The flame of recidivous libido brought them back to the exciting ardor of former youth, and they set snares for the unfortunate woman's integrity. (4) They are really ravishers of purity who feign love but harbor only hate in their hearts. She resists them and they threaten her with false accusations. Adulterers themselves, they have the audacity to appear as denouncers of adultery. (5) Trapped between these two menacing cliffs of wantoness, she cried to the Lord for help because her body lacked the strength to restrain them. The Lord from heaven heard purity calling to Him. Completely crushed by injustice and being led to her punishment, she saw the penalty imposed upon her enemies. Though she had found herself so often in deadly peril, she emerged victress twice: over death and over lust. (6) It would be endless were I to give you more examples. I am satisfied with these two because the case for purity has there been vigorously defended.

Chapter 10

The unwelcome thought of noble lineage, which for some is an incentive to lewdness, could not soften their resolution,[1] nor did a

3 Cf. Gregory of Elvira, *Tractatus Origenis* 5, lines 24-62 (ed. Bulhart, CCL 69.35-36).

1 Cf. Dan. 13.

1 For chs. 10, 11, 12 (opening), cf. Gregory of Elvira, *op. cit.* 5, lines 66-121 (CCL 69.36-37).

beautiful body and a well-proportioned figure corrupt them. Such comeliness frequently produces the impression that, this being like the flower of youth which quickly passes away, advantage should be taken of any pleasure that present itself. The early years of budding and maturescent youth had no adverse effect on them. During this period, young hot blood enkindles the raging heats of nature and sets in motion the blind passions that dwell in the very marrow of the bones, seeking relief for itself even at the endangerment of modesty. Opportunity for concealment, without witnesses, did not allure them, though this often exerts an overpowering force for the perpetration of crime when there is a prospect for impunity through acquittal. Neither pressure from the authority of those who commanded them nor the boldness afforded by accomplices and conspirators—though often good intentions are broken down by such things—could make them yield. Gifts, which even good men often accept, allegations, threats, suffering, even death could not weaken them (2) Nothing [was deemed] so barbarous, so unbearable, so distressing as the abandonment of the sublime standards of purity. (3) In the divine judgment they were found so deserving of reward that one was honored with an all but regal throne; the other was reconciled with her husband and compensated by the death of her enemies. (4) We should keep these and similar examples before our eyes and meditate on them day and night.

Chapter 11

A consciousness of spotless modesty gives incomparable delight to the faithful soul. The greatest pleasure is mastery of pleasure itself. No victory is greater than victory over one's inordinate desires. (2) A man is stronger than the man he overcomes; however, he does not overcome himself, but another. He who represses lust overcomes himself. He who defeats an adversary overcomes an alien agent, but the man who banishes inordinate desires overcomes an enemy of his own household. (3) Man can more readily cope with any other evil than sensual pleasure. Evil, whatever be its nature, always inspires horror; sensual pleasure is always alluring. We overcome nothing with more difficulty than that which we love precisely because it harms us. (4) Since fear arises from inordinate desires, the man who discourages inordinate desires banishes also fear. (5) He who withstands inordinate desires is victorious over sin. The man who overcomes inordinate desires is superior to the world itself. He who <overcomes inordinate desires> proves that he is a true disciple of Christ. He who <overcomes inordinate desires> shows that he has crushed underfoot an ancient evil which infects the entire human race. He who masters inordinate desires wins for himself lasting peace. He who overcomes inordinate desires regains freedom of mind—something very difficult even for the freeborn. (6) Therefore, brethren, we should always, as the facts indicate, practice purity. That this virtue may be the easier of attainment it is based on no acquired skills. (7) What brings it to fulfillment is the will; if the will is lacking, all else is of no avail. It appertains to our own will. We have nothing to acquire but only to cherish what is already ours.

Chapter 12

What else is purity but a wholesome attitude that serves as the body's custodian, to the end that modesty, owed to the sexes and sealed by a certain severity, might, through an untarnished offspring, preserve the uprightness of the race? (2) Holy meditation on the precepts, a soul prone to faith, a mind completely dedicated to holy religion, and especially the fear of God are recognized, brethren, as things closely allied with purity. Modesty strives to avoid anything that is beyond measure, improper, extravagant, artfully made-up, and meretriciously devised either to offend or to attract attention. (3) The woman who tries to win anothers's affection is not a modest woman, even though she remains physically intact. There is no place for the woman who strives, not merely to enhance, but to prostitute her loveliness. To be overly concerned about one's beauty is in itself a flaw and indicative of an imperfect spirit. (4) One should not tamper with the nature of one's body nor violate the handiwork of God. That woman will always be miserable who is not content to be what she really is. Why is the hair dyed? Why is shadow applied to the extremities of the eyes? Why is the face artfully moulded into a different shape? Finally, why does she make use of a mirror? Isn't it because she is afraid to be herself? (5) The attire of a modest woman should also be modest. The faithful soul, in her choice of colors, should not make use of anything that smacks of adultery. When a woman interweaves her clothing with gold, it's as if she thought it of value to corrupt her vesture. What are stiff metals doing among the delicate threads of the woven fabric? These metals only weigh down drooping shoulders and expose the wantonness of an unhappily proud spirit. (6) Why are women's necks concealed and loaded down with imported stones whose cost, exclusive of jeweler's fee, exceed an entire fortune? [1] Such women do not adorn themselves—they merely make a show of their own vices. (7) With their fingers and ankles adorned with gold, is it any wonder that they cannot move about? [2] Is all this merely fashionable or is it just a pompous showcase of one's patrimony? (8) What irony! To think that women, who are so delicate in everything, are superior to men when it comes to shouldering the burden of their vices.

Chapter 13

But, to get back to what I began with, men and women must both have great regard for purity and keep within its boundaries with all watchfulness. Purity is always in jeopardy because of the body's inclinations; the flesh forever tends downwards and can carry purity along with it. (2) One can make the excuse that nature itself stirs up in man those desires by which the ruins of a fallen people are restored. She uses the blandishments of pleasure to deceive, not leading her protégés into the propagation of progeny of legitimate embrace but hurling them into sin. (3) Therefore we must struggle with every kind of virtue against the wiles of the flesh whereby the devil artfully creeps in as ally and guide. (4) Let your conduct be Christlike, as the Apostle admonishes. The spirit should, as much as possible, restrain the flesh. One's frame of mind should be far removed from things of the flesh. Correct your faults so that you will always detest them. Always keep before your eyes how de-

1 Cf. Tertullian, *The Apparel of Women* 1.9.3 (tr. by E.A. Quain, FC 40.128).
2 Cf. Isa. 3.16-21.

basingly and disgustingly shameful sin is. Penitence,[1] with all the grief it entails, is shameful evidence of sins committed. (5) Do not look too inquisitively into the faces of strangers. Your speech should be measured and your laughter contained. Laughter betrays an easygoing and dissipated spirit. Even virtuous contacts are to be avoided. When it is a matter of avoiding sins of the flesh, grant the body nothing. Think often how virtuous it is to overcome moral turpitude and how base it is to be overcome by it.

Chapter 14

I must also say that adultery is not pleasure but mutual reproach. Whatever brings death to the soul and destroys modesty cannot possibly give delight. (2) The spirit must discipline the sting of the flesh. It must curb the violent impulses of the flesh. The spirit has received the power at will to bring under subjection the members of the body. The spirit, after a manner of speaking, like a tried and true charioteer, curbs with the reins of the heavenly precepts the impetus of the flesh which exceeds the just limitations of the body. For it fears that the chariot of the body when driven beyond its limits will dash to destruction both itself and its charioteer. (3) When such things happen—better, even before such things happen—you must seek divine assistance against all disturbances and against all short-comings. Only God who deigned to created man is powerful enough also to give man adequate assistance. (4) I have not written much because it was not my intention to write a book—only to give a brief exhortation. As for yourselves, examine the Scriptures. Glean from their teaching better illustrations on this matter for yourselves. Dearest brothers, fare you well.

1 Cf. W. Le Saint, *Tertullian: On Penitence* (ACW 28.132-33 n. 10).

LETTERS

INTRODUCTION

HESE PAGES SUPPLEMENT the brief treatment of
Novatian's correspondence found above in the General
Introduction.

When Pope Fabian died in prison during the Decian persecution
(January 20, A.D. 250), Novatian handled the correspondence between Cyprian, Bishop of Carthage, and the presbyteral college
(*presbyterium*) of Rome that had assumed direction of the Christian
community there until the election of a new bishop. Most of this
correspondence has perished, but three letters to Cyprian survive
whose composition is now with good reason attributed to Novatian,[1] all three written in the year 250 and probably in the months
of August and September.[2] The letters are all concerned with an
urgent problem that then faced the Christian communities and especially those of Rome and Carthage—how to deal with those who had
lapsed during the persecution and now sought renewal of communion with the Church. Questions had come in this matter from
Cyprian, to which Letters 1 and 3 contain the replies made by
Novatian in the name of the Roman presbyters and deacons. The
lapsed were to be admitted to penance; however, the duration and
the conditions of that penance were not to be determined until a
community which, like Rome, had lost its bishop should elect one.

---

1 For Novatian's authorship of Letter 1 we have the testimony of Cyprian
himself (*Ep.* 55.5; tr. by Sr. Rose Bernard Donna, C.S.J., FC 51.136).
Evidence from style and content clearly proves Letter 3 to be by the same
hand (see below, at n. 22 and Diercks CCL 4.ix n. 12), and the similar case
for Letter 2 is hardly weaker (see below at nn. 13, 22 and Diercks, *loc.
cit.*).
2 See Diercks, CCL 4.xii.

If the lapsed were in danger of death, they were to be pardoned.[3] These two letters openly manifest the strong rigorist convictions at which Novatian arrived in stressing the ancient tradition of strictness in the Roman Church.[4] However, we must observe with C. B. Daly: "Novatian professed in his rigoristic pronouncements to speak for the Church of Rome; but his claim was rigorously opposed, in the name of tradition, by the moderate party among the presbyters."[5]

Novatian made no distinction between the gravity of the sin of the *libellatici* and that of the *sacrificati* (Christians who had actually offered sacrifice to the gods).[6] Furthermore, Daly observes that the word *evangelium* and the adjective *evangelicus*, repeatedly found in these two letters, are always used in the sense of strictness.[7] Novatian states that reconciliation can be granted to the lapsed in danger of death, but he manifests a certain reluctance to grant pardon and insists that it must be granted only in the sinner's last moments.[8] He uses the word *severitas* (severity) three times in Letter 1 and once in Letter 3.[9] He uses the word *vigor*, which has the meaning there of "rigor," "severity," and "discipline," five times in Letter 1 and once in Letter 3.[10] One readily observes Novatian's predilection for the scriptural text: "Whoever disowns me before men I will disown him before my Father in heaven."[11]

We find this same stern strain echoed in Letter 2, written in the person of a group of Roman confessors (named and unnamed)[12] and

---

3 *Ep.* 1.8.–P.F. Palmer, *Sacraments and Forgiveness* . . . (Sources of Christian Theology 2; Westminster, Md., and London 1961) 40, makes this observation: "The policy of the Roman clergy formed during the vacancy of the Roman see is confirmed by neighbouring and distant bishops who have sought refuge in Rome," and (p. 42) cites Novatian, *Ep.* 1.8.

4 *Ep.* 1.2 (CCL 4.200); *Ep.* 3.3 (CCL 4.249).

5 C. B. Daly, "Novatian and Tertullian: A Chapter in the History of Puritanism," *Irish Theological Quarterly* 19 (1952) 34.

6 *Ep.* 1.3 (CCL 4.201-2); see Daly, *op. cit.* 36. For the Latin terms, see *Ep.* 1 n. 3.

7 Daly, *op. cit.* 36 n. 5.

8 *Ep.* 1.6 (CCL 4.204); cf. *Ep.* 3.1 (CCL 4.247-48).

9 *Ep.* 1.2-4 (CCL 4.200-202); *Ep.* 3.1 (CCL 4.247). See Melin, *op. cit.* 62.

10 *Ep.* 1.1-4 (CCL 4.200-202); *Ep.* 3.1 (CCL 4.247). See Melin, *op. cit.* 61-62; Daly, *op. cit.* 36 n. 9.

11 Matt. 10.33; *Ep.* 1.7 (CCL 4.205).

12 This letter begins: *Inter varios* . . . and is found in Diercks, CCL 4.227-34.

all but certainly by Novatian's hand. [13] In this letter he uses the word *censura*, which has the meaning there of "punitive judgment," "blame," and "severity"; it also appears twice in Letter 1. [14] "What will happen to the fear of God," writes Novatian, "if pardon is so readily granted to sinners?" [15] The pardon of the lapsed "must be handled with prudence and moderation." [16]

The tone of Novatian's three letters is decidedly more severe and harsher than Cyprian's conciliatory tone. Yet both Cyprian and Novatian had been influenced by Tertullian, so much so that Cyprian's manner of referring to the Carthaginian polemicist as "the master" can also apply to Novatian. Cyprian. however, avoided Tertullian's rigorism; unfortunately, Novatian did not. In his struggle with the laxist party championed by Felicissimus, Cyprian saw a precious ally in the severity of the Roman presbyteral college, represented by Novatian, who, in his own struggle against the moderate party at Rome, felt flattered that the illustrious Cyprian shared his views. [17] Later Cyprian sided with Pope Cornelius and adopted the latter's less rigoristic position. [18] Novatian remained uncompromising.

At the end of the fourth century, Bishop Pacian of Barcelona had recourse to Novatian's Letter 1 to refute the Novatianist Sympronian. The latter had sent the bishop his four opuscula in defense of the strictness of his sect. Pacian replied that Novatian, before he had become antipope, had written that the lapsed who were seriously ill and in danger of death were to be granted peace and reconciliation. If the Novatianists refused to grant pardon and reconciliation to the

---

13 Melin, *op. cit.* 43-67.
14 *Ep.* 2.6 (CCL 4.232); *Ep.* 1.1, 7 (CCL 4.200, 205); Daly, *op. cit.* 36 n. 9.
15 *Ep.* 2.6 (CCL 4.232).
16 *Ibid.*
17 Diercks, CCL 4.x.
18 Cyprian, *Ep.* 55.4-7 (FC 51.135-38); Diercks, *loc. cit.* Cyprian's position may be conveniently studied in Maurice Bévenot, S.J. (ed. and tr.), *Cyprian: De Lapsis and De Ecclesiae Unitate* (Oxford 1971), esp. pp. vii-x, 1-55 (text and annotated English translation of the *De lapsis*), 100-22 (excerpts from *Epp.* 55 and 59 in translation), 127 (*s.v.* Novatian).

lapsed, argued Pacian, it can only mean that the founder of the sect had contradicted himself.[19]

The practice of penance in the early Church is still the subject of heated controversy. There is considerable difference of opinion between Church historians, on the one hand, and dogmatic theologians on the other. Although there is universal insistence on the practice of penance and reconciliation for sins committed after baptism, the precise manner of dealing with grave sins in the early Church requires further research.[20]

The style of Novatian's letters is elegant, as the skillful use of various figures attests.[21] J. Schrijnen and C. Mohrmann distinguish the style of Letters 1 and 3, which they label "kulturlateinisch," from the manner of writing called "vulgärlateinisch" in Letter 2.[22]

The present translation is based on the critical texts of W. Hartel, CSEL 3.2 (1871), L. Bayard (Paris 1925), and G. F. Diercks, CCL 4 (Turnhout 1972).

* * * * *

The manuscript of the present work was already in the hands of the printer when there became available a work of fundamental importance for the correspondence of St. Cyprian: Luc Duquenne, S. J., *Chronologie des lettres de S. Cyprien: Le dossier de la persécution de Dèce* (Subsidia hagiographica 54; Brussels 1972). It has not been possible, therefore, to make detailed references to this book, but it may be noted here that pp. 28-33, 97-89, 135-40, 158-65 are relevant to Novation.

19 Pacian, *Ep. ad Sympronianum Novatianum* 3.5 (PL 13.1067B); cf. Novatian, *Ep.* 1.8 (CCL 4.205-6).
20 See F. X. Murphy, "Penitential Controversy," NCE 11 (New York 1967) 85.
21 For example, anaphora appears at *Ep.* 2.1 (CCL 4.227-28) and *Ep.* 1.7 (CCL 4.205); antithesis at *Ep.* 1.7 (CCL 4.205).
22 J, Schrijnen and C. Mohrmann, *Studien zur Syntax der Briefe des hl. Cyprian* 2 (Nijmegen 1937) 107-8 (cited by G. F. Díercks, CCL 4.ix n. 12). The Nijmegen scholars were writing, however, before Melin's *Studia* (1946); see above, n. 13.

SELECT BIBLIOGRAPHY

Texts:

Bayard, L. (ed., tr.). *St. Cyprien, Correspondance* 1 (Paris 1925) 71-83, 89-92.
Diercks, G. F. *Novatiani opera . . .* (CCL 4) 181-252.
Hartel, W. CSEL 3.2 (1871) 549-64, 572-75.

Translations:

Baer, J. in *Bibliothek der Kirchenväter* 60 (Munich 1928) 90-106, 114-18.
Donna, Sr. Rose Bernard, C.S.J. *St. Cyprian. Letters,* FC 51.72-84, 90-94.
Wallis, R. E. in *Ante-Nicene Fathers* 5 (New York 1899) 302-05, 307-11. Here our *Ep.* 2 is called [Cyprian,] *Ep.* 25, and our *Epp.* 3 and 1, [Cyprian,] *Epp.* 29 and 30 respectively.

Secondary Sources:

Bévenot, M. "A Bishop is responsible to God alone (St. Cyprian)," *Recherches de science religieuse* 39 (1951/52) 397-415.
Daly, C. B. "Novatian and Tertullian," *Irish Theological Quarterly* 19 (1952) 33-44.
Duquenne, L., S.J. *Chronologie des lettres de S. Cyprien: Le dossier de la persécution de Dèce* (Subsidia hagiographica 54; Brussels 1972). [See above, p. 182.]
Melin, B. *Studia in Corpus Cyprianeum* (Uppsala 1946) 79-88.
Pincherle, A. "Sulle origini del cristianesimo in Sicilia," *Kokalos* 10-11 (1964/65) 547-62.
Quasten, J. *Patrology* 2.226.

*In all the works here listed (except Wallis's translation, *q.v.*) the three letters of Novatian are cited as *Epp.* 30, 31, 36 in the correspondence of Cyprian.) In PL 4 the three letters are numbered 31, 26, 30 respectively in Cyprian's correspondence.

CONTENTS

LETTER 1

(Ep. 30 in St. Cyprian's correspondence)

The presbyters and deacons serving at Rome send their greetings to Bishop Cyprian.

Chapter 1

HE MAN WHO IS CONSCIOUS of having acted well and relies upon the strength of evangelical discipline and who can testify to himself of his fidelity to the divine law is usually content to have God as his sole judge. He neither seeks the praise of others, nor fears their accusations. They are deserving of double praise, however, who wish their actions to have the approval of their brethren, even though they know quite well that they are held responsible to God alone, their judge.[1] (2) We are not in the least surprised that you, brother Cyprian, are acting in such a manner. With your customary modesty and innate zeal, you have wished us to be participants in, not judges of, your policies so that our approval of your undertakings would also make us co-sharers with you in their glory. When we subscribed to your deliberations, we would become fellow beneficiaries. One can readily conclude that all of us have equally collaborated in these deliberations because he will find all of us united and of one mind in regard to discipline and censure.

---

1 For the impact of this passage on Cyprian, see M. Bévenot, "A Bishop is responsible to God alone (St. Cyprian)," *Recherches de science religieuse* 39 (1951/52) 397-415.

Chapter 2

Is there anything that could be more fitting in time of peace, or more necessary during the strife of persecution than to maintain the due strictness of divine discipline? It is quite evident that the man who relaxes the strictness of this discipline forever drifts about haphazardly on an unsteady course and finds himself tossed about hither and yon by the unforseeable vicissitudes of events. Once the rudder of counsel has been wrenched, as it were, from his hands, he will run the ship of the Church's welfare on the rocks. Certainly, there is no better way to provide for the welfare of the Church than by standing up against those who infringe upon it, as one would do against oncoming waves, and one must cling to the norms of discipline which have always been observed, as one would hold fast to a rudder for safety in a storm.

(2) We have not just recently adopted this particular course of action, nor have these measures against the ungodly suddenly crossed our mind. For with us, the strictness is ancient, the faith is ancient. The Apostle would not have praised us so highly by stating: "Your faith is spoken of throughout the whole world,"[2] if this strictness of ours had not already been rooted in the faith of those times. To fall from the pinnacle of such praise and glory is the greatest of misfortunes. It is less inglorious never to have achieved public esteem than to topple from its summit. It is less blameworthy never to have been honored by a glorious testimonial, than to have lost the honor of glorious testimonials. It is less <prejudicial>never to have had one's merits recognized, to remain unknown and without esteem, than to be stripped of the heritage of one's faith and of the praise it brings. If one does not painstakingly and solicitously live up to what has been said in one's praise, then it all takes the swollen form of hatred for a grave crime.

Chapter 3

That we speak the truth is evident from our previous letters. In them, we have given you a clear explanation of our position against

2 Rom. 1.8.

those who have revealed themselves as nonbelievers by an unlawful show of those despicable certificates of sacrifice.[3] They seem to think that by such action on their part, they can avoid the treacherous snares of the devil. But the very fact that they claim to have offered sacrifice makes them no less guilty than if they had actually stepped before those iniquitous altars. In our letters we have also expressed ourselves against those who had acquired receipts even though they were not personally present when they were acquired. You can be sure that their presence was felt when they ordered those receipts to be drawn up in a specified manner. The man who has issued the orders for the perpetration of crime is not free of guilt. Although one did not actually commit the crime, he is certainly no stranger to crime, if he consents to have a document, attesting to the commission of the crime, read publicly. Since the entire mystery of faith is contained in the confession of the name of Christ, the man who seeks by deceptive stratagems to exempt himself has already denied Christ. Likewise, the man who wants to give others the impression of having obeyed edicts and laws, promulgated contrary to the Gospel, has, in effect, obeyed them simply because he wanted others to believe that he had already obeyed them.

(2) We have expressed our convictions in this matter—and we thereby support your position—against those who have polluted their hands and their mouths by taking part in unlawful sacrifices. Since their hearts had already been polluted, their hands and mouths were thereby also polluted. (3) Far be it from the Church at Rome to set aside her austerity by assuming a worldly and overly indulgent manner and, in undermining the strength of her discipline, to completely ruin the majesty of her faith. If now, when so many of our lapsed brethren lie powerless on the ground—and still continue to succumb—one were to apply with undue haste remedies which will only prove ineffectual in the long run for their reconciliation, and, moved by a sense of false mercy, one were merely to add new

3 There were various classes of apostates or lapsed: the *sacrificati*, who had actually offered sacrifice to the gods; the *thurificati*, who had burned incense before the gods; the *libellatici*, who had not actually sacrificed but had secured, by bribery or other means, a *libellus* or written statement (certificate) that they had offered sacrifice.

wounds to the old wounds of apostasy, then these unfortunate people are deprived even of penitence, to their greater detriment. What can indulgent treatment possibly accomplish if even the physician himself is adverse to penitence and favors the danger if he merely covers the wound and does not give it the necessary time to form a scar? If we were to speak candidly, such treatment does not cure the patient—it kills him.

Chapter 4

Furthermore, you have received a letter,[4] which is in agreement with ours, from the confessors who are still being detained here in the dungeons for their magnificent confession. Their faith, already manifested once before in open confession, has gloriously crowned them for their struggle on behalf of the Gospel. In this letter, they have upheld the strictness of evangelical discipline and have vindicated the honor of the Church against the inroads of indiscreet requests which they could not encourage without seriously undermining evangelical discipline. Who could be more obligated to safeguard the continuity of evangelical severity with untarnished dignity than they who have surrendered themselves to infuriated persecutors to be tortured and racked for the sake of the Gospel? They suffered all these things for fear that they would lose the crown of martyrdom, which they unquestionably would have lost if they had chosen, on the occasion of their martyrdom, to become apostates from the Gospel. The man who does not carefully watch over the source of what he possesses, loses what he has already acquired through injuring the prime source of what he possesses.

Chapter 5

At this point, we must express our great debt of gratitude to you and thank you for brightening up the gloom of their prison with your letters. You visited with them as best you could. Your letters

---

4 Cf. Cyprian, *Ep.* 28.2 (tr. Sr. Rose Bernard Donna, C.S.J., FC 51.70).

and consoling words gladdened hearts, strong in the confession of their faith. When you lauded their good fortune with fitting praise, you inflamed them with a very ardent longing for heavenly glory. Encouraging the downcast, you have, through the force of your words, stimulated those who, we firmly believe and hope, will soon be victors. Though all this appears to spring from work of divine grace and the faith of the confessors, they are, undoubtedly, indebted in their martyrdom to you to some extent.

(2) But let us return now to the subject of our discussion. You will find herewith a copy of the letter that we have also sent to Sicily.[5] Indeed, we have a more pressing need to postpone this matter in that, after the death of Fabian[6] of very revered memory, the circumstances and the vicissitudes of our times have not permitted us to appoint a new bishop who can take care of all these matters and reckon with the question of the lapsed with authority and sound judgement.

(3) We are pleased with your treatment of this very difficult matter: one must first wait until peace has returned to the Church and only then, after having taken counsel with the bishops, presbyters, deacons, confessors, and the remaining faithful laity, proceed to deal with the case of the lapsed.[7] We find it extremely odious and irksome that a large number of people does not pass judgment on a crime that seems to have been perpetrated by a large number, and issue a joint resolution, since such an enormous crime manifestly is widespread among many. A resolution which does not have the support of a large number has no substance.

(4) Look at the whole world, almost completely devastated, and the wrecks and the ruins of the fallen strewn about! Therefore, the situation demands a policy in keeping with the prevalence of the transgression. The medicine must be commensurate with the wound, the remedies equal to the deadly destruction. Those who fell, fell because a blinding and foolish boldness overpowered them and

5 Cf. A. Pincherle, "Sulle origini del cristianesimo in Sicilia," *Kokalos* 10-11 (1964/65) 547-62.
6 See above, Introduction, near beginning.
7 Cf. Cyprian, *Ep.* 55.5 (tr. Donna, FC 51.136).

rendered them too incautious. Therefore, the people who attempt to put this whole matter to rights must use the greatest moderation in counsel, lest an unwise resolution be judged by all as of no effect.

Chapter 6

Accordingly, we who seemingly have eluded, at least for the time being, the calamities of this period, as well as those who have actually fallen into this disaster, should now, with one mind, one prayer, one lament, implore the Divine Majesty to grant peace to the Church. Let us have recourse to mutual prayer, that we may cherish, watch over and arm one another. (2) Let us pray for the lapsed that they may be lifted up. Let us pray for those who remain steadfast that in their hour of trial they may not fall. Let us pray for those who are reported to have fallen, that they may acknowledge the magnitude of their sin and realize that their predicament requires something more than just a cursory or precipitate treatment. Let us pray that the indulgence granted to the lapsed may be followed by their penitence and that, realizing the full extent of their crimes, they may patiently bear with us for the time being. May they not in any way disturb the troubled condition of the Church, lest they ignite an intestine persecution among us and crown their crimes with restlessness.

(3) A sense of shame especially befits those in whose sins a shameless attitude is censured. Let them, indeed, knock at the door, but they are not to break it down. Let them take their stand at the threshold of the Church, but they are not to leap over it. Let them keep watch at the portals of the heavenly camp, but they are to fortify themselves with that self-restraint by which they may see that they have been deserters. Let them take up once again the trumpet and sound their requests, but the sound should not be the call to battle. They should, indeed, arm themselves[8] with the weapons of self-restraint, and let them take up once again the shield of faith, which they had discarded when they committed apostasy for fear of death. They should realize, however, that they are armed

---

8 For the military metaphors in this passage, cf. Eph. 6.13-17.

now to wage war against their enemy, the devil—not against the Church, which grieves over their fall. A modest petition, an unpretentious request, coupled with an indispensable humility and a patience that is not idle will be of great profit to them. Let them send tears as ambassadors of their sufferings. May the sobs which rise from the depths of their heart serve as advocates for them, giving proof of the sorrow and shame they feel for the crime committed.

Chapter 7

Indeed, if they are truly horrified at the magnitude of the dishonor that they have brought down upon themselves, if they were to probe with a physician's hand the lethal blow to their heart and conscience with its deep and sinuous recesses, they would be ashamed even to ask for reconciliation, were it not that not to have sought the assistance of peace puts one once more in greater danger and carries with it a greater stigma. But all this is to be done in the Sacrament,[9] according to the regulation for the request itself, within the limits of the proper time. The demand should be modest, the request, subdued, one should bend, not irritate anyone from whom reconciliation is sought. One must take into consideration, not only divine clemency, but also divine severity. For as it is written: "I forgave you all the debt, because you did entreat Me";[10] so is it also written: "Whoever disowns Me before men, I will also disown him before My Father and before His angels."[11]

(2) God is compassionate, but He also demands—indeed, He strictly demands—the observance of His precepts. He invites guests to His wedding banquet, but the man who wears no wedding garment He

9 The term "sacrament" is the English equivalent of the Latin *sacramentum*; it was also one of the ways in which the Greek word for "mystery" was rendered. It had many meanings in Scripture and early Christian writings, but two concepts are basic: *a sacred secret* and *its manifestation*. See J. R. Quinn, "Sacraments, Theology of," NCE 12 (New York 1967) 806. Throughout the *Trinity* of Novatian, it has the meaning of "mystery," "prefiguration," "prophecy"; cf. Mohrmann, in *Vigiliae Christianae* 3 (1949) 170-71 (*Etudes sur le latin des chrétiens* 3.114). Here *sacramentum* may refer to the sacrament of penance.
10 Matt. 18.32.
11 Matt. 10.33; Luke 12.9.

has cast out by his hands and feet from the assembly of the saints.[12] He has prepared heaven, but He has also prepared Tartarus. He has prepared refreshment, but He has also prepared eternal punishment. He has prepared inaccessible light, but He has also prepared the desolate and eternal darkness of perpetual night.

Chapter 8

In our endeavors to steer a middle course in these difficult matters, we—indeed, many of us in conjunction with some of the neighboring bishops as well as other bishops who were driven here from distant provinces by the fury of the persecution—came to the conclusion some time ago that there is to be no innovation before the election of a Bishop. We believe, however, that the treatment of the lapsed is to be handled with discretion. Meanwhile, however, while we wait for God to give us a Bishop, the cases of those who can bear to wait should be kept in abeyance. But those of the lapsed whose death is imminent and who can suffer no delay, after they have manifested their repentance and repeatedly and openly declared their abhorrence of what they have done, and if they have given signs of genuine sorrow and repentance by their tears, their sighs, their sobs, and when there remains, as far as we can humanly ascertain, no hope of life, then and only then are they to be aided with the proper care and solicitude.[13] God knows what to do with them and how to balance the scales of His justice. We, however, take great care that we not be prone to a too ready pardon for wicked men to praise, but that, on the other hand, the truly penitent may not accuse us of what they think to be an inflexible cruelty.

Most fortunate and illustrious Bishop, fare you well in the Lord— such is our prayer—and think of us.

---

12 Cf. Matt. 22.13. For the "inaccessible light" just below, cf. 1 Tim. 6.16.
13 Reconciliation normally took place with the imposition of the hand and the prayer of the bishop or a priest; this gave the lapsed person the right to partake of the Eucharist.

LETTER 2

(Ep. 31 in St. Cyprian's correspondence)

The priests, Moses and Maximus, as well as Nicostratus and Rufinus[1] and the other confessors who are with them, send their greetings to Bishop Cyprian.

Chapter 1

Although we find ourselves overwhelmed, brother, by the manifold and various sorrows caused by the recent lapse of so many brethren throughout almost the entire world, the greatest of consolations was afforded us upon the receipt of your letter,[2] which not only gave us courage but also assuaged somewhat the bitterness of our sorrow. From that letter we can now comprehend the favor of Divine Providence which willed us confined to prison for so long a time and, perhaps, for no other reason than that, with a more earnest will, we might be able to attain the crown destined for us, after having been admonished and greatly encouraged by your letter. (2) This brought light in upon us, being like a calm in a storm, a longed-for tranquillity in a raging sea, rest in labor, health amid pain and danger, a bright and radiant light in the densest gloom. Our parched mind completely imbibed and received it with hungry longing. We rejoice that we have been sufficiently fed and nourished by it for our struggle with the enemy.

(3) The Lord will reward you for your charity and will grant you a well-deserved recompense for this excellent deed. The person who

---

1 These Roman confessors were very active in the controversy over the lapsed. At first they sided with Novatian (cf. Cyprian, *Ep.* 46 [FC 51.118-19]); later they returned to the Church. Moses died a martyr. Nicostratus went with Novatus (see FC 51.68 n. 12) to Carthage. Since here, as in *Ep.* 1 and 3, Novatian writes as the representative of the Roman clergy, the presence in the salutation of the names of Moses and the others does not militate against the (now all but established) authorship of Novatian.

2 According to Baer and Bayard, Novatian alludes to Cyprian, *Ep.* 20, addressed to the priests and deacons of Rome.

merely exhorted others is not less worthy of the reward of a crown than one who suffered. The person who instructed others is not less worthy of praise than one who actually carried out the instructions. The person who admonished others is not to be honored less than one who was filled with ardent longing. In fact, it is usually the teacher who enjoys greater renown than does the pupil, be he ever so docile. For perhaps the latter would never have accomplished what he actually did, unless the former had had that which produced the effect.

Chapter 2

We repeat, therefore, brother Cyprian, that we experienced great joy, great comfort, great relief, because you described with becoming high praise, I do not say the glorious deaths, but rather the glorious immortality of the martyrs. Deaths of this sort had to be represented in such language that the first-hand reports were so retold as to square with the actual happenings. Thanks to your letter, we witnessed the glorious triumphs of the martyrs. Our eyes followed them, as best they could, entering heaven, and we contemplated them, as it were, seated among the angels, the powers and the celestial dominations. (2) In some sort of manner, moreover, our ears heard the Lord rendering the witness that He promised to give them before the Father.[3] This is what raises our spirits with each passing day and inflames us with the desire to attain to such heights of glory.

Chapter 3

What more glorious or happier fate could possible befall any man with the help of divine grace than to confess without fear and in the midst of his tormentors the Lord God? What could be more glorious than to confess Christ, the Son of God, amid the most diverse and most exquisite tortures of a cruel, secular power? The body is racked, lacerated, stripped of its flesh, but the spirit, even though it

3 Cf. Matt. 10.32; Luke 12.8.

is leaving the body, still remains free. What could be more glorious than to quit the world for heaven, to leave men behind and to be among the angels, to break all worldly ties and to stand disencumbered in the presence of God, to obtain the kingdom of heaven without delay? What could be more wonderful than to become, with one's confession of the name of Christ, a partner with Christ in His Passion, and to be made, because God deigns it so, a judge of one's own judge? What could be more glorious, after one has confessed the name of Christ, than to come away with an unstained conscience, to refuse to obey human and sacrilegious laws against the faith, to bear public witness to the truth, in dying to conquer death dreaded by all, to gain immortality through death itself, to overcome every torment by enduring the torments of the rack and the dismemberment of one's body by all the instruments that man's cruelty can devise? What could be more glorious than to withstand all the sufferings of an excruciated body with unflinching spirit, not to fear the draining of one's blood, to begin, after having confessed the faith, to love one's sufferings, to consider it a detriment to one's real life to live any longer?

Chapter 4

The Lord urges us to this battle when, with the trumpet of His Gospel, He says: "Whoever loves father or mother more than me is not worthy of me;[4] and he who loves his soul more than me is not worthy of me,[5] and he who does not take up his cross and follow me, is not worthy of me."[6] Again He states: "Blest are those persecuted for holiness' sake; the kingdom of heaven is theirs. Blest are you when they persecute you and hate you. Be glad and rejoice because they persecuted the prophets before you in the very same way."[7] He also says: "You will be brought to trial before kings and governors. Brother will hand over brother to death, and the father

4 Matt. 10.37.
5 *Ibid.*; cf. Luke 14.26; cf. also Matt. 10.39; 16.24-25.
6 Matt. 10.38.
7 Matt. 5.10-12.

his child, but whoever holds out till the end will escape death."[8] (2) And He adds: "I will give the victor the right to sit with me on my throne, as I myself won the victory and took my seat beside my Father on His throne."[9] The Apostle also says: "Who will separate us from the love of Christ? Trial, or distress, or persecution, or hunger, or nakedness, or danger, or the sword? As Scriptures says: 'For your sake we are being slain all the day long; we are looked upon as sheep to be slaughtered.' Yet in all this we are conquerors because of Him who has loved us."[10]

Chapter 5

When we read these and similar passages in the Gospel, they act as so many torches applied by the words of the Lord to kindle our faith. We do not fear the enemies of truth—we even provoke them! Because we have not submitted to them, we have vanquished the enemies of God and their abominable laws against the truth. If we have not yet shed our blood, we are ready to shed it. No one must think that the stay, which has been granted us, is an act of clemency, because it only harms us, it is a real hindrance to glory, it delays heaven, it holds us back from the vision of God. In a struggle of this kind, and in the sort of contest where one's faith takes part it is true clemency not to put off the martyrs by granting them a stay.

(2) Dearest Cyprian, beseech the Lord that, with the passing of each day, He may more abundantly and more generously arm and enlighten us with His grace. May He strengthen and fortify us with the fullness of His power so that He, as the best of commanders, may now lead forth to the prepared battleground those soldiers of His whom He has heretofore trained and tested in the proving grounds of their prisons. May he furnish us with divine arms,[11] truly invincible weapons: "the breastplate of justice"[12] which is never broken, "the shield of faith"[13] which cannot be pierced, and "the

8 Matt. 10.18, 21-22; Mark 13.9, 12-13.
9 Rev. 3.21.
10 Rom. 8.35-37.
11 Cf. Eph. 6.13.
12 Eph. 6.14; cf. 1 Thess. 5.8.
13 Eph. 6.16.

ct that they are numerous; they are the more to be curbed be-
use they are not few in number. The sheer number of offenders
ually contributes nothing toward the extenuation of a crime. What
ally counts is a feeling of shame, self-restraint, penitence, disci-
ine, humility, and submission; a willingness to await others' judg-
ent on one's self and to accept the sentence that others pass on
ne's own conduct. (4) This is the proof of penitence. This is what
rings healing to a deep wound, uplifts and elevates a dejected mind,
ssuages and puts an end to the feverish ardor of seething transgres-
ions. The doctor does not prescribe for the sick food which healthy
people can enjoy, for fear that the wrong diet will only aggravate,
not check, the ravages of ill-health, or that an ailment which could
have been cured much sooner by abstinence will drag on because the
impatient patient suffers from an overstuffed stomach.

Chapter 7

Hands which have been soiled by impious sacrifice must be
cleansed by good works. Wretched lips polluted by food offered to
idols must be purified with words of genuine penitence, and in the
depths of one's being one must sow the seeds of a new and devout
spirit. Let the repeated lamentations of the penitents be heard and
let devout tears flow from eyes which have looked upon idols with evil
intent. With tears that are acceptable to God, let those eyes delete the
wrong they have perpetrated. (2) There is no place for impatience in
time of sickness. Sick people wrestle with their pain in hope that
their patient endurance will overcome the pain and eventually win
good health for them. A wound which has been cicatrized too
hastily by the doctor is insecure, and the healing will give way at the
slightest mischance if faithful use is not made of the healing brought
by time itself. A small flame will quickly break into open conflagration, unless the fuel of the entire fire is extinguished down to the
last spark. The people of whom we are speaking should realize that
even the postponements which they endure are really to their interest and that delays are indispensable for the working of a surer cure.

Chapter 8

Why is it that those who confess Christ have to languish behind
bars in filthy prisons, if they who have denied Him have done so
without imperiling their standing among the faithful? Why is it that

sword of the spirit"[14] which has never been damaged.
we bid to request these weapons for us, if not so gloric
Should not victims destined to be sacrificed request
of the priest?

Chapter 6

Another source of joy for us is the manner in which
out your episcopal duties. Although you were torn awa
brethren for a time because of prevailing conditions, you r
them. Your letters were a source of frequent encouragem
confessors. You even defrayed their necessary expenses by
your own legitimate labors. Everyone could somehow al
your presence. In all your duties, you never fell behind, as
is wont to do.

(2) We cannot be silent about the overwhelming joy tha
forcibly stirred up in us; in fact, we cannot help but grant
testimony that our voice can command. We have observed h
have reprimanded with justifiable severity both those who, u
ful of their transgressions, have too hastily and overeagerly e
reconciliation from the presbyters in your absence, and tho
who, without regard for the Gospel, have too readily given aw
holy of the Lord and the pearls.[15] A crime of such magnitude
has laid waste with incredible destruction almost the entire
must be handled, as you yourself write, with prudence and
eration. All the bishops, presbyters, deacons, confessors, and
laity who have remained faithful are to be consulted, as you sta
your letters, lest unsuitable efforts to brace what is falling into
lead to more serious collapse.

(3) What will happen to the fear of God if pardon is so read
granted to sinners? One must train their minds and nourish the
allowing them time to reach full development. From Scripture th
are to be instructed that they have committed a heinous sin—o
that surpasses all other sins. They should not find comfort in th

14 Eph. 6.17.
15 Cf. Matt. 7.6.

the confessors are bound in chains for the name of God if the lapsed who have refused to confess God are allowed participation in the communion of the Church? To what purpose do they who are detained in prison lay down their glorious lives if they who have abandoned their faith do not feel the magnitude of their dangers and of their transgressions? (2) When they show excessive impatience and demand intolerable haste in their efforts to obtain reconciliation, in vain do their saucy and unbridled tongues spit out querulous and hateful remonstrances which are to no avail against the truth, since they might have retained in their own right what now under a compulsion of their own seeking they are driven to demand. Faith which was capable of confessing Christ was also capable, with the help of Christ, of remaining in communion.

We hope, most blessed and glorious Father, that you will always fare well in the Lord and be mindful of us.

LETTER 3

(*Ep.* 36 in St. Cyprian's correspondence)

The presbyters and deacons serving at Rome send their greetings to Bishop Cyprian.

Chapter 1

After reading the letter[1] that you, dearest brother, sent us with the subdeacon Fortunatus,[2] we were stricken with a double grief, perplexed with a double sorrow, both that the trials and tribulations of the persecution have given you no respite and that you indicated that the immoderate petulance of the lapsed brethren had been carried to the point of dangerous and foolhardy language. (2) Although we were greatly troubled by the aforementioned state of affairs, the firmness and the strictness which you have displayed in keeping with evangelical discipline have lightened our heavy burden of grief. On the one hand, you restrain, with good right, the improbity of some of them; on the other, your exhortations to penitence point out the way of lawful salvation. Indeed, we are amazed

1 Cyprian, *Ep.* 35 (FC 51.89-90).
2 A subdeacon of Carthage, cf. Cyprian, *Ep.* 34.4 (FC 51.89).

that they have reached the point where, at an unseasonable and difficult time and notwithstanding the commission of a heinous sin, a monstrous crime, they do not simply beg for reconciliation but lay claim to it with the greatest insistence; rather, they say that they have already obtained it in heaven.

(3) If they have obtained it, why do they demand what they already possess? If, however, the very fact that they demand it proves that they do not have it, then why do they not await the judgment of those from whom they thought it proper to ask for the reconciliation which they actually do not have? But if they believe that they have the prerogative of communion from any other source, let them try to relate it to the Gospel, so that thus finally it may be firmly established, if there is no disharmony with the Gospel precepts. For how can what has been determined contrary to the truth of the Gospel possibly afford a communion that is in accord with the Gospel? Every prerogative ultimately looks to a privilege of special consideration, if one is not out of harmony with the person with whom he wishes to be associated. Conversely, if one is out of harmony with the person with whom he wishes to be associated, he necessarily forfeits the special consideration and privilege of association.

Chapter 2

Therefore, let them reflect on just what they intend to accomplish in this matter. If they say that the Gospel lays down one rule of conduct and the martyrs another, then, they will incur a double danger by placing the martyrs at variance with the Gospel. On the one hand, the authority of the Gospel will be destroyed and brought low, if it could be superseded by the innovation of another decree; on the other, the glorious crown of their confession will topple from the heads of the martyrs, if they are found not to have attained it by the observance of the Gospel, which makes martyrs. No one should be more careful to abstain from a decision contrary to the Gospel than the person who is struggling to receive the name of martyr from the Gospel.

(2) We would like to ascertain one other thing. If the martyrs

became martyrs for no other reason than to keep their peace with the Church through refusing to offer sacrifice, even to the shedding of their blood, fearing lest, overcome by the pain of torture, they lose this peace and thereby their own salvation, how, then, could they think that salvation should be granted to those who had sacrificed, when they knew full well that they themselves would have forfeited this same salvation if they had offered sacrifice? The law which they had previously applied to themselves also holds for others. (3) In this matter, we notice that they brought forward against themselves the course of action they thought worked in their favor. If the martyrs thought that peace was to be granted to the lapsed, why did not they themselves grant it? Why were they of the opinion that the case was to be referred to the bishop, as they themselves say? The person who orders something to be done, can also do what he orders to be done. But as we know—or, better, as the whole matter speaks for itself and proclaims—our most holy martyrs thought that a certain measure of self-restraint and consideration for the truth should be shown on both sides. Since they were under pressure from many, in sending the lapsed to the bishop, they thought that they must consult their own modesty so as to avoid further entreaties. In refusing to communicate directly with the lapsed, they made it clear that the purity of the evangelical law must be kept intact

Chapter 3

You, brother, in your charity, never cease to calm the spirits of the lapsed and to proffer the medicine of truth to those in error, even though the ailing mind commonly rejects the physician's solicitous care. The wound of the lapsed is still fresh and still swelling. Therefore, we are certain that when they have been given more time to recover and their excessive impatience has waned, they will appreciate postponement for the purpose of receiving reliable treatment. If only those who stir them up to their peril were wanting! These men give them bad instruction and, instead of the salutary remedy of delay, demand for them the fatal poison of a hasty reconciliation. (2) We do not believe that all of the lapsed would have so vehemently dared to demand reconciliation for themselves without the instigation of certain people. We know the faith of the Church of Carthage; we know of its practice; we know of its humility. Hence we were amazed to find in a letter[3] certain harsh remarks written against you, since we are well aware of your charity for one another, which shines forth in many instances of mutual affection.

(3) It is time, then, for them to do penance for their transgression, to manifest genuine sorrow for their fall, to show self-restraint, humility, and modesty, so that they may elicit God's clemency in their behalf by their submission and draw down upon themselves divine mercy by treating God's bishop with becoming deference. How much more efficacious their letters would have been if they had only subjoined their own humility to the intercession of those who remained faithful! A request is more readily granted, when the person for whom the request is made is worthy to receive what is asked.

Chapter 4

With regard to Privatus of Lambaesis,[4] you acted as you usually do in wishing to inform us of the matter as causing anxiety. We must all watch over the body of the entire Church, whose members are scattered throughout all the many provinces.[5] (2) Even prior to the reception of your letter, we were well aware of the deceit of that crafty man. A certain Futurus,[6] a member of that wicked band, came here some time ago as a standard-bearer for Privatus and attempted fraudulently to obtain a letter from us. He could not hide his identity and he did not get the letter he wanted.

We wish that you may always fare well.

---

3 It is unclear why Baer and Bayard (*ad loc.*) refer here to [Cyprian,] *Ep.* 23.
4 Privatus was the former bishop of Lambaesis in Numidia. He was condemned for heresy by Donatus, Cyprian's predecessor as bishop of Carthage. Cf. *Ep.* 59.10 (FC 51.181).
5 Cf. Cyprian, *The Unity of the Church* 5 (tr. Bévenot, *op. cit.* [Intr. n. 18] 67).
6 The use of Futurus as a proper name in Africa is questioned; Pamelius thought that Futurus and Felicissimus were the same person; see Sr. Rose Bernard Donna, in FC 51.93 n. 3 and Baluze's note on [Cyprian,] *Ep.* 30 (=36) in PL 4.307D.

INDICES

GENERAL INDEX

207

Muratorian Fragment, 13
Murphy, F. X., 182 n.
"mystery," 193 n.
Mysterium Fidei, 117 n.

nabla, 124, 125
nativitas, 109 n.
Nativity, 46, 53, 80, 83
Nature, 30 n.
NeoCaesarea, Council of, 4
Neoplatonic philosophy, 27 n.
Neusner, J., 151 n.
newt, 149
Nicaea, Council of, 9, 23 n.
Nicostratus, 185, 195
nightjar, 150
Noah, 39, 64, 147
Novatian, importance in theology, 1, 13; name, 1-2; birth, 2; early years, 2; character, 3-4; baptism, 2-3; priesthood, 3; role in church, 1, 179; "episcopal consecration," 4-5; antipope, 1, 4; his concept of the church, 5; attitude toward the lapsed, 5-6, 179-82; later years, 6; question of possible martyrdom, 6-7; inscription honoring a martyr Novatian, 7; spread of his schismatic church, 8-9; extant and nonextant works, 7-8, 138
The Trinity, theological importance, 13-14; date of composition, 14; doctrine, 14-19; original title, 23 n.; translated, 23-111; references to, 1, 7, 9 n., 13, 14, 26 n., 131 n., 144 n., 160 n., 193 n.

The Spectacles, composition and scope, 115-18; translated, 123-33; references to, 7, 8, 115 n., 160, 166 n.
Jewish Foods, sources, 137; content, 138; translated, 143-56; references to, 7 n., 9 n., 14 n., 115, 137, 138, 139, 151 n., 155 n., 159, 160
In Praise of Purity, purpose and content, 159; authorship, 159-60; style, 160; translated, 165-76; references to, 7, 8, 103 n., 115, 159
Letters, authorship, 179 n.; rigoristic tone, 180-82; style, 182; translated, 187-204; references to, 1 n., 5 n., 7, 9 n., 179 n., 180 n., 181 n., 195 n.,
Novatian, martyr at Rome, possibly distinct from the antipope, 6-7
Novatian, martyr at Cordova, 6
Novatianist(s), 6, 8, 9, 102 n., 181
Novatus, priest of Carthage, 2, 195 n.

Origen, 13, 77 n., 148 n.; *see also* Gregory of Elvira
ostrich, 150
Ovid, 26 n.

Pacian, bishop of Barcelona, 6, 181, 182
Paffroet, R., 160

INDEX OF HOLY SCRIPTURE

(Books of the Old Testament)

(BOOKS OF THE NEW TESTAMENT)

Index

THE FATHERS
OF THE CHURCH

(A series of approximately 100 volumes when completed)

translated by L. Schopp
The Magnitude of the Soul
translated by J. McMahon
On Music
translated by R. Taliaferro
The Advantage of Believing
translated by L. Meagher
On Faith in Things Unseen
translated by R. Deferrari, M–F. McDonald

OCLC 856032

Volume 5:   SAINT AUGUSTINE   (1948)
The Happy Life
translated by L. Schopp
Answer to Skeptics *(Contra Academicos)*
translated by D. Kavanagh
Divine Providence and the Problem of Evil
translated by R. Russell
The Soliloquies
translated by T. Gilligan

OCLC 728405

Volume 6:   WRITINGS OF SAINT JUSTIN MARTYR   (1948)
The First Apology
The Second Apology
The Dialogue with Trypho
Exhortation to the Greeks
Discourse to the Greeks
The Monarchy or Rule of God
translated by T. Falls

OCLC 807077

Volume 7:   NICETA OF REMESIANA   (1949)
Writings of Niceta of Remesiana
translated by G. Walsh
Prosper of Aquitaine: Grace and Free Will
translated by J. O'Donnell
Writings of Sulpicius Severus
translated by B. Peebles
Vincent of Lerins: The Commonitories
translated by R. Morris

OCLC 807068

Volume 8:   SAINT AUGUSTINE   (1950)

The City of God (books 1–7)
translated by D. Zema, G. Walsh

OCLC 807084

Volume 9:   SAINT BASIL ASCETICAL WORKS   (1950)
translated by M. Wagner

OCLC 856020

Volume 10:   TERTULLIAN APOLOGETICAL WORKS   (1950)
Tertullian Apology
translated by E–J. Daly
On the Soul
translated by E. Quain
The Testimony of the Soul
To Scapula
translated by R. Arbesmann
Minucius Felix: Octavius
translated by R. Arbesmann

OCLC 1037264

Volume 11:   SAINT AUGUSTINE   (1957)
Commentary on the Lord's Sermon on the Mount
Selected Sermons (17)
translated by D. Kavanagh

OCLC 2210742

Volume 12:   SAINT AUGUSTINE   (1951)
Letters (1–82)
translated by W. Parsons

OCLC 807061

Volume 13:   SAINT BASIL   (1951)
Letters (1–185)
translated by A–C. Way

OCLC 2276183

Volume 14:   SAINT AUGUSTINE   (1952)
The City of God (books 8–16)
translated by G. Walsh, G. Monahan

OCLC 807084

Volume 15:   EARLY CHRISTIAN BIOGRAPHIES   (1952)
Life of St. Ambrose by Paulinus
translated by J. Lacy
Life of St. Augustine by Bishop Possidius

Life of St. Cyprian by Pontius
  translated by M. M. Mueller, R. Deferrari
Life of St. Epiphanius by Ennodius
  translated by G. Cook
Life of St. Paul the First Hermit
Life of St. Hilarion by St. Jerome
Life of Malchus by St. Jerome
  translated by L. Ewald
Life of St. Anthony by St. Athanasius
  translated by E. Keenan
A Sermon on the Life of St. Honoratus by St. Hilary
  translated by R. Deferrari

OCLC 806775

Volume 16:　　　　　SAINT AUGUSTINE　　　　　(1952)
The Christian Life
Lying
The Work of Monks
The Usefulness of Fasting
  translated by S. Muldowney
Against Lying
  translated by H. Jaffe
Continence
  translated by M–F. McDonald
Patience
  translated by L. Meagher
The Excellence of Widowhood
  translated by C. Eagan
The Eight Questions of Dulcitius
  translated by M. Deferrari

OCLC 806731

Volume 17:　　　SAINT PETER CHRYSOLOGUS　　　(1953)
Selected Sermons
Letter to Eutyches
　　　　　　　SAINT VALERIAN
Homilies
Letter to the Monks
  translated by G. Ganss

OCLC 806783

Volume 18:　　　　　SAINT AUGUSTINE　　　　　(1953)

Letters (83–130)
translated by W. Parsons

OCLC 807061

Volume 19:   EUSEBIUS PAMPHILI   (1953)
Ecclesiastical History (books 1–5)
translated by R. Deferrari

OCLC 708651

Volume 20:   SAINT AUGUSTINE   (1953)
Letters (131–164)
translated by W. Parsons

OCLC 807061

Volume 21:   SAINT AUGUSTINE   (1953)
Confessions
translated by V. Bourke

OCLC 2210845

Volume 22:   FUNERAL ORATIONS   (1953)
Saint Gregory Nazianzen: Four Funeral Orations
translated by L. McCauley
Saint Ambrose: On the Death of His Brother Satyrus I & II
translated by J. Sullivan, M. McGuire
Saint Ambrose: Consolation on the Death of Emperor
Valentinian
Funeral Oration on the Death of Emperor Theodosius
translated by R. Deferrari

OCLC 806797

Volume 23:   CLEMENT OF ALEXANDRIA   (1954)
Christ the Educator
translated by S. Wood

OCLC 2200024

Volume 24:   SAINT AUGUSTINE   (1954)
The City of God (books 17-22)
translated by G. Walsh, D. Honan

OCLC 807084

Volume 25:   SAINT HILARY OF POITIERS   (1954)
The Trinity
translated by S. McKenna

OCLC 806781

Volume 26:   SAINT AMBROSE   (1954)

Letters (204–270)
        translated by W. Parsons

                                                    OCLC 807061

Volume 33:   SAINT JOHN CHRYSOSTOM   (1957)
        Commentary on St. John The Apostle and Evangelist
        Homilies (1–47)
                translated by T. Goggin

                                                    OCLC 2210926

Volume 34:   SAINT LEO THE GREAT   (1957)
        Letters
                translated by E. Hunt

                                                    OCLC 825765

Volume 35:   SAINT AUGUSTINE   (1957)
        Against Julian
                translated by M. Schumacher

                                                    OCLC 3255620

Volume 36:   SAINT CYPRIAN   (1958)
        To Donatus
        The Lapsed
        The Unity of the Church
        The Lord's Prayer
        To Demetrian
        Mortality
        Works and Almsgiving
        Jealousy and Envy
        Exhortation to Martyrdom to Fortunatus
        That Idols Are Not Gods
                translated by R. Deferrari
        The Dress of Virgins
                translated by A. Keenan
        The Good of Patience
                translated by G. Conway

                                                    OCLC 3894637

Volume 37:   SAINT JOHN OF DAMASCUS   (1958)
        The Fount of Knowledge
        On Heresies
        The Orthodox Faith (4 books)
                translated by F. Chase, Jr.

                                                    OCLC 810002

The Sacrament of the Incarnation of Our Lord
The Sacraments
translated by R. Deferrari

OCLC 2316634

Volume 45:   SAINT AUGUSTINE   (1963)
The Trinity
translated by S. McKenna

OCLC 784847

Volume 46:   SAINT BASIL   (1963)
Exegetic Homilies
translated by A–C. Way

OCLC 806743

Volume 47:   SAINT CAESARIUS OF ARLES II   (1963)
Sermons (81–186)
translated by M. M. Mueller

OCLC 2494636

Volume 48:   THE HOMILIES OF SAINT JEROME   (1964)
Homilies 1–59
translated by L. Ewald

OCLC 412009

Volume 49:   LACTANTIUS   (1964)
The Divine Institutes
translated by M–F. McDonald

OCLC 711211

Volume 50:   PAULUS OROSIUS   (1964)
The Seven Books of History Against the Pagans
translated by R. Deferrari

OCLC 711212

Volume 51:   SAINT CYPRIAN   (1964)
Letters (1–81)
translated by R. Donna

OCLC 806738

Volume 52:   THE POEMS OF PRUDENTIUS   (1965)
The Divinity of Christ
The Origin of Sin
The Spiritual Combat
Against Symmachus (two books)
Scenes from Sacred History Or Twofold Nourishment
translated by C. Eagan

Volume 59:   SAINT AUGUSTINE   (1968)
     The Teacher
     The Free Choice of the Will
     Grace and Free Will
          translated by R. Russell
                                        OCLC 712674

Volume 60:   SAINT AUGUSTINE   (1968)
     The Retractations
          translated by I. Bogan
                                        OCLC 712676

Volume 61: THE WORKS OF SAINT CYRIL OF JERUSALEM I (1969)
     Procatechesis
          translated by A. Stephenson
     Lenten Lectures 1–12 (Catecheses)
          translated by L. McCauley
                                        OCLC 21885

Volume 62:   IBERIAN FATHERS I   (1969)
     Writings of Martin of Braga
          Sayings of the Egyptian Fathers
          Driving Away Vanity
          Exhortation to Humility
          Anger
          Reforming the Rustics
          Rules For An Honest Life
          Triple Immersion
          Easter
     Paschasius of Dumium
          Questions and Answers of the Greek Fathers
     Writings of Leander of Seville
          The Training of Nuns and the Contempt of the World
          Sermon on the Triumph of the Church for the Conver-
          sion of the Goths
          translated by C. Barlow
                                        OCLC 718095

Volume 63:   IBERIAN FATHERS II   (1969)
     Braulio of Saragossa
          Letters of Braulio
          Life of St. Emilian
          List of the Books of Isidore of Seville
     Writings of Fructuosus of Braga

Rule for the Monastery of Compludo
General Rule for Monasteries
Pact
Monastic Agreement
translated by C. Barlow

OCLC 718095

Volume 64:　　THE WORKS OF SAINT CYRIL　　(1970)
　　　　　　　OF JERUSALEM II
Lenten Lectures (Catcheses) 13–18
　translated by L. McCauley
The Mystagogical Lectures
Sermon on the Paralytic
Letter to Constantius
　translated by A. Stephenson

OCLC 21885

Volume 65　　　　SAINT AMBROSE　　　(1972)
Seven Exegetical Works
　Isaac or the Soul
　Death as a Good
　Jacob and the Happy Life
　Joseph
　The Patriarchs
　Flight from the World
　The Prayer of Job and David
　translated by M. McHugh

OCLC 314148

Volume 66:　　SAINT CAESARIUS OF ARLES III　(1973)
Sermons 187–238
　translated by M. M. Mueller

OCLC 1035149; 2494636

Volume 67:　　　　NOVATIAN　　　　(1974)
The Trinity
The Spectacles
Jewish Foods
In Praise of Purity
Letters
　translated by R. DeSimone

OCLC 662181